The BOND

PEOPLE AND

The BO

SIMON & SCHUSTER EDITIONS

Essays by Roger A. Caras

THEIR ANIMALS

ND

Photographs by Shel Secunda

to our wives,

Jill Caras

and

Victoria Secunda,

and in

memory of

Charlie Powell

SIMON & SCHUSTER EDITIONS
Rockefeller Center
1230 Avenue of the Americas
New York, NY 10020

Designed by Jim Wageman, Wigwag

Manufactured by Butler & Tanner Limited, Great Britain
10 9 8 7 6 5 4 3 2 1

Library of Congress Cataloging-in-Publication Data
Caras, Roger A.
    The bond: people and their animals / essays by Roger Caras;
photographs by Shel Secunda.
        p.   cm.
        1. Pets—United States—Anecdotes. 2. Pet owners—United
States—Interviews. 3. Celebrities—United States—Interviews.
4. Human–animal relationships—United States—Anecdotes.
5. Pets—United States—Pictorial works. 6. Pet owners—United
States—Pictorial works. 7. Celebrities—United States—Pictorial
works. I. Secunda, Sheldon. II. Title.
SF416.C37   1997
636.088'7—dc21   97-17616
                                                          CIP

ISBN 0-684-83082-5

c o n t e n t s

introduction

ROGER A. CARAS

$\mathcal{I}$T IS ALMOST IMPOSSIBLE to talk about human beings and their relationships with other species without pitching headfirst into a veritable maelstrom of clichés. That is not because animal lovers think or feel in clichés, but rather because our language is woefully lacking in the words we need to describe what we feel. Phrases or expressions like "unconditional love" and "nonjudgmental love" are accurate enough and do at least indicate what most people believe is going on in their relationships, but they fall short of really exploring or describing the phenomena. They touch on it, but no more than that.

Even without enough language to work with, we still should try to convey what is happening when humans and animals bond. Consider the historical perspective. Before agriculture, before fabrics and metal, computers, space travel, electricity, before plastics and medicine, the printing press and television, before architecture and automobiles, popcorn or coffee, people had companion dogs in the cave. They extracted them from the wolf, a species as social as their own. People had always lived near wolves, but now they began keeping them and breeding them and thus derived the dog from their genes.

Aside from the natural biological functions of our own bodies, little of our life today is akin to that lived in the cave except for the fact that we keep animals. Making companions of other species is one of the very oldest things we do. Fire is older, chipped stone tools are older, but almost nothing else is. Having a pet is a natural part of being a human being.

Clearly, if we have been keeping pets for fourteen or fifteen thousand years—through hundreds of generations— there must be something extraordinary to it. It obviously feels good, but is that all? A great many modern medical studies reveal a whole spectrum of survival advantages that pet owners experience, such as lower blood pressure, fewer and milder heart attacks and reduced stress. That could keep a social habit in place for millennia, with pet owners in each generation living long enough to pass the idea along to their progeny. And, indeed, that appears to be what happens. The majority, but not all, the pet owners or animal lovers (they are close to being synonymous) in this book come from pet-owning or animal-loving families. Although these pages concentrate on individual people with individual pets, many of these people own more than one pet, and the pet or pets belong to more than one person—belong in the sense that they are loved by other people in the household. It is obviously a terrific family thing to do. It is one of the easiest sharing things a family can experience.

Not owning a pet does not seem to preclude love of them. When Shel Secunda, the amazing photographic part of this team, and I began compiling lists of possible subjects and asking for suggestions from our friends, we found a large number of people who would have been fun to interview and interesting to photograph who did not have pets at that moment. "My dog died last year," one of the greatest living playwrights told me, and we met with that sort of response again and again. One of the leading newsmen in television today declined to participate because his dog is fifteen years old and, although well loved, "doesn't look healthy and happy anymore." A highly respected actress who was to be part of our cast lost her dog to old age a few days before the scheduled photo session. For the majority of the petless people we encountered, petlessness was a temporary state. One very famous scientist keeps her dogs in England, and many people talked about pets they had had in the past (we included only one of them, Joe Garagiola, because his story is so nice); most were simply living in a style that didn't allow for pets at the moment. Almost all of the people we encountered have, have had or intend to get pets soon.

The people who did join our cast were invited to do so because they represent an intriguing diversity (ages, for example, run from ten to ninety-four), because they have fascinating and often touching stories to tell and because, obviously, they are interesting and articulate people who talk easily of their relationship to the animals in their lives. We are grateful to all of them. Putting it simply, it was fun being with them and sharing their enthusiasm.

Shel Secunda and I decided to join forces on this book very shortly after we first met. We weren't old friends when we began, but we are now—not because the book took a long time to complete, but because Shel is the easiest collaborator, and the funniest, I have ever worked with on a project of any kind.

It is the usual practice when giving acknowledgments at the beginning of a book to state that any errors are the fault of the author. In this case that wouldn't be accurate. They are all Shel's. I am grateful to him anyway. Animal people, and he is one of them, in or out of this book, are the nicest people I know.

—*Thistle Hill Farm, Freeland, Maryland*

introduction

SHEL SECUNDA

AT THE RISK OF OVERSTATEMENT, never has the boredom of a German shepherd had so profound an effect on the course of a person's career. When I posed my ferocious-looking dog, Brim, with an infant and he suddenly

yawned, he provided me with this image that inexorably altered my professional life—the photograph was selected for the permanent collection of the International Center of Photography. Even more significantly, it convinced me of the singular pleasure of photographing people together with their animals.

I began my career as an advertising and editorial photographer, with people as my primary focus of interest. Within a short time, I found myself including animals in my photographs whenever possible—the shots seemed somehow incomplete without them. Eventually, I started getting cranky when asked to do a photo *without* an animal in it. That realization was the genesis of this book.

Although I had a dog, I was by no means an authority on animals, so I called Roger Caras, whom I knew slightly. Talk about starting at the top! When he agreed to be my partner on the project, I was ecstatic. Certainly, no one is more qualified to write about the people-animal connection than Roger.

Creative collaborations can be challenging at best, horrendous at worst. After a year of almost daily telephone conversations and mutual submissions of our work for approval or comment, I'm happy to say that we are closer friends than ever.

Photographing people and animals together is unlike photographing either alone—in some ways easier and in other ways more complex. On the easy side, when being photographed with their favorite pets, vanity on the part of human subjects is rare. The most glamorous celebrities often become outrageous muggers, completely abandoning any concerns about how good they look.

One of the complexities of photographing people and pets together, however, is the animal's occasional reluctance to pose. With dogs, the offer of a treat or the distraction of my barking at *them* will usually induce canine cooperation and an alert or quizzical facial expression.

Cats, being more independent creatures, are another story altogether. My session with Carol Burnett was particularly memorable. The amount of time Carol and her cat spent in front of the camera was brief; the time Carol and I spent on our hands and knees trying to coax the feline fugitive out from under Carol's bed was a good deal longer.

The kind of portraiture I do entails certain hazards, such as bites or scratches, which I accept as perils of the profession. But in the case of two animals in this book, my anxiety levels spiked. Although Tippi Hedren was utterly serene cradled in the curl of her African bull elephant Timbo's trunk, I had never before been in close proximity to such a huge animal without sturdy bars between me and it.

Only one of my animal subjects required that I take drastic protective measures. Susan Goldstein described Mac, her sun conure—a member of the parrot family—as a "man-eater." Forewarned that the robin-sized bird could, and probably would, with a single chomp, draw blood, I caged myself in a large corrugated cardboard box, my lens protruding through a small opening. Only then was Mac released from his own cage, flying to perch atop Susan's head.

I owe a great debt to the forty-six people and their animal friends who graciously made their time and faces available to me. For assistance in assembling our cast, I am grateful to Nadine Brozan, Neil Hickey, Pat and Ray Hoesten, Marguerite and Bob Jones, Susan Klein, Stacy Nusbaum, Anne Scott, Cookie and Shelly Steinmetz, and Gretchen Wyler. Bill McCann and his staff at Putnam Imaging Center in Danbury, Connecticut, unfailingly produced exceptional negatives and prints with promptness, courtesy and professionalism. Special thanks to Arthur Cantor for giving me the chance, long ago, to learn that I was a better photographer than theatrical publicist.

In addition, there are three others who helped to make this project an absolute joy. Elaine Markson, my literary agent, is exactly who I would have gotten had it ever occurred to me that the way to find a great agent is to pray for one. Gillian Casey Sowell edited my work with an invaluable blend of critical comment and enthusiastic support, inspiring me to keep trying to top myself.

And last, but light-years from least, the person who taught me that good enough is never good at all and who sets a standard of perfection in her writing and in just about everything else she does that I can only aspire to: my wife, Victoria Secunda, whose only grumble about our respective professions is the vast number of words she must produce to match the alleged worth of one measly click of my shutter.

— *Ridgefield, Connecticut*

The BOND

james earl jones

*J*AMES EARL JONES longs to have some pigeons of his own, and it seems certain that before long he will. First, he loves animals, and second, one has only to review his stage and film career to realize that this man with the voice of a god (and Darth Vader) does pretty much what he wants to do, sooner or later.

James was born on a farm in Mississippi, the son of an actor-prizefighter, Robert, but lived there for only four and a half years. Though short, that stay engendered fond memories of horses, cows, pigs, rabbits, goats, ducks, geese, dogs and guinea fowl. His discussion of that period is full of enthusiastic expressions like, "That kid was the prettiest little billy I have ever seen." The course was set. James Earl Jones would never willingly be without animals.

Before he was five, James moved to Dublin, Michigan. The big day came when he was twelve. His own "personal dog" arrived in Dublin, shipped up to him from his mother in St. Louis. That airedale was to be the first of many dogs, because the man with the most recognized voice in America has seldom been without a dog of his own since that day. There were family dogs, of course, notably a shepherd, but the "personal dog" was always special.

After he had graduated from the University of Michigan and served as a lieutenant in the army, James moved to New York. His first dog in the city was a basset. By the time his career really took off and he achieved star status, the desire to get back to the land became a dominant force in shaping his lifestyle; the family got a country place, along with horses. The travel demands that were being made on the young actor were too great for the gentleman-farmer role to be realistic, however, and the horses all went to good homes. There will be more horses in the future but, unlike the pigeons, they will have to wait until James's thirteen-year-old son, Flynn, outgrows his horse allergy, something the doctors are sure he will do.

James muses, "We never had a dog that bit anyone. I guess that's because of the way we treat them." Of special memory is Liver—also called Leather—who was a weimaraner-terrier cross. One terrible day he was killed by a car, and James buried him on the farm. James recalls sadly that Liver was his favorite dog of all time.

An early favorite had been James's second personal dog, Rusty. He died violently, too, back in Michigan. One day in late fall, Rusty made the mistake of challenging a buck. In breeding prime, the angry deer gored him to death. Now the Joneses' dogs dwell behind a buried electric fence. They are allowed to feel as if they are in charge on home turf, but they are protected from their impulse to sally forth and look for trouble.

Today, Patches is the resident dog at the country home of James, Ceci and Flynn Jones. He is a year-and-a-half-old Staffordshire bull terrier mix. The dog that some people call a "pit bull" and fear, can be—and is, in Patches's case—a close and loving friend. He was found on a golf course in California, the victim of heaven alone knows what mischance. A relative of James's took him in, but over a period of time it was clear that Patches was never so happy as when James came to visit. Patches bonded to Ceci and Flynn as well as he had to James and is now part of the family.

For as long as he lives, Patches will play a special role in a special household. He has, James claims, an unusually wide selection of vocalizations (it must run in the family!). With a variety of whines, moans, groans and barks he expresses his delight and his displeasure. His greatest displeasure comes when he sees suitcases come out of the closet as frequently they must. His greatest delight is when the members of the Jones clan are home where they belong.

James Earl Jones clearly loves Patches, and when you are with this great man, feeling his presence, listening to his amazing voice, you believe that he would somehow be less complete, less the full-fashioned person he is if he were denied his "personal dog."

It will be interesting to see what pigeons will add.

annemarie lucas

ANNEMARIE is the only person who was interviewed for this book while wearing a bulletproof vest and with a 9 mm Smith & Wesson, handcuffs and pepper spray hanging from her belt. At five feet three inches and a hundred and twelve pounds, Annemarie, once an actress, is now a cop of a special kind.

There have always been animals in Annemarie's life. Her parents are animal lovers, and she came by it naturally.

"For my entire life I have had dogs," she says. "When I was growing up we had cats, gerbils, guinea pigs, birds, rabbits, but always a dog. Dogs have always been there for me, there was such camaraderie. We grew up together. I don't think I could live without an animal in my life."

Today, Annemarie and her husband, Richard, have four male cats, Shaney, Benny, Mako and Cody, who is seen here, as well as a dog that was a stray when she found it. For the time being their dog has to live with Annemarie's parents in Maine. Both Annemarie and Richard have very demanding careers.

As a young actress, Annemarie was making ends meet by modeling. On a shoot in New York, she became caught up in a mini-riot triggered by an NBA draft. That was when she met Richard, who was a member of the police task force responding to the disturbance. He called a week later, they dated and then she popped the question: How did he feel about animals? He confessed that he was an animal lover, and the match was made. She laughs now, because, "He said he didn't want a cat when we got married—he's a dog person—but somehow we now have four cats and he loves them fervently. He's worse than I am about them."

Annemarie was uncertain about her acting career, how far she wanted to go with it. She wondered about it a great deal and had a lot of doubts.

"I used to pray to God, 'Just let me find what I am supposed to be.' I always wanted to be different, to make a difference, to help, to be able to do something I am good at. I measure people by how good they are at helping the world. That's why I fell in love with Rich," she says.

The answer to Annemarie's prayers came from Rich. He is a sergeant with the elite Harbor Patrol of the New York City Police Department. He is doing the two things he loves most: being a good, hardworking police officer and working on the water. He was Annemarie's role model. He encouraged her to become an officer too. She applied to the Humane Law Enforcement Division of the ASPCA and passed the demanding physical requirements in spite of her diminutive size.

"I love this job," she says. "Every time you take an animal out of a horrible situation, it is the best feeling imaginable—knowing that you stopped the suffering. I have more passion for this than I ever had for acting, no comparison. Acting is, well, acting, and this is real life. It is far more exciting. Being around Rich and his friends sparked my interest in law enforcement. Now, I understand his job and he certainly understands mine. He helps me out by advising me how to handle tough situations.

"Every day is a different challenge. You never know what is going to happen out there, and of course, I am around animals. Sometimes I am nervous, I've even been scared. There have been two incidents where men became very aggressive when I was alone in an investigation. I had to put out a 10-85 both times—a call for backup. The ASPCA guys and the city police both responded."

And how are the two careers within one marriage working out?

"I think we are the two happiest people in New York City. We drive in together in the morning, and we giggle. We really do, we love what we are doing so much. Rich is on the water, that's his ambition, and I'm with my animals. It's almost too good to be true."

red buttons

RED BUTTONS'S first real experience with the animal kingdom did not bode well for a meaningful relationship. As a very little boy on Manhattan's Lower East Side he got bitten by what he remembers as a very large dog. The experience left more than a physical scar. He says, "If I saw a dog a block away, I froze. I would duck into a doorway. That's the way I grew up." Red's feelings did not change until years later. "When I was twenty-one, I was in burlesque, and I went on the road for a six-month tour. My straight man had a boxer named Gretchen that traveled with him. I was terrified of her. I called my agent and told him to get me out of the tour. There was no way I was going to travel with a dog. He couldn't or wouldn't do it, and my straight man was not about to get rid of the dog. After about two weeks, he said, 'Look, Red, calm down. Look at the way she is looking at you. She loves you.' So I calmed down and by the end of the tour I was walking her all the time. I was crazy about her, and she loved me."

Other animals besides dogs played a part in the professional life of actor-comedian Red Buttons. He recalls, "It was in 1960–61, we were shooting *Hatari* in Africa. It looked like the Bronx Zoo with the cages open. It was an amazing experience—all kinds of animals. I was doing a scene with John Wayne. All of a sudden, a leopard comes walking out of the bushes. Duke says, 'Buttons, see what he wants.'"

Red also points out, "I was on Broadway, if you want to talk about real animals." But that, obviously, is a different story.

Red's true complete conversion to loving dogs came with another love. He explains, "What really, really, *really*, did it was when I started going with Alicia [they have been married for thirty-three years]. She came up to my apartment with her two poodles. One immediately made a mess on my rug. I said it was going to be me or them, and then she told me who was going to win that one. I settled down and really did come to love those little dogs. Now, we have six—three poodles, a Chihuahua, a Lhasa apso and a Labrador."

And how many horses does Alicia have? Buttons raises his eyebrows. "If you find out, tell me."

Does Red ride too?

"When I was sixteen, I was working in the Catskills [as a stand-up comic]. It was during the Depression, and I was being paid $1.50 a week. There was a stable across the road from the hotel, and I wanted to learn to ride, so I hung around there. But it cost $1.00 an hour to rent a horse. At my salary, that was out of the question. The guy who ran the place had seen my act, though, and offered me free riding. It was nice, and I got to be really good. One day he says to me: 'Why do you want to be an actor? They're a dime a dozen. You'll starve. Be a jockey. I can make you into a jockey. You'll make a fortune throwing races.' I told him I would have to ask my mother. He told me to forget the whole thing."

When you talk to Red Buttons, after his sixty-two years as a professional comic and both comedic and dramatic actor, it can be a little difficult to know exactly when he is pulling your leg and when he is serious. About one thing, though, you can be certain of his genuine feelings. For Red and his wife, Alicia, the companionship of animals, especially dogs, is the perfectly normal way of life. One suspects that Red would no longer know what it would be like to even try to live any other way. The little boy from the Lower East Side, terrorized by a dog so long ago, has become a real dog person.

gretchen wyler

*W*HEN SHE WAS GROWING UP in Bartlesville, Oklahoma, Gretchen Wyler didn't have much of a feel for animals. There were some family dogs, but she doesn't remember them. All she cared about was becoming a ballerina.

Gretchen can turn anything into a happening—her entrance into a room is a theatrical event, when she sneezes, forget it! She made it onto Broadway while in her teens. There were eight Broadway shows, including some that will never be forgotten such as *Guys and Dolls, Silk Stockings, Damn Yankees* and *Bye, Bye Birdie,* as well as *Sweet Charity* in London's West End. They molded Gretchen in the Broadway tradition of the triple-threat performer with starring roles on television, in films and on stage. But something besides her own burning ambition had come to life.

In 1960, her husband of those years, cellist Shepard Coleman, wanted a dog, specifically a Great Dane. Gretchen was appearing at the Shubert in *Bye, Bye Birdie,* and although she had no idea what it would be like to live with a dog, she said "Sure, why not?" To humor her husband she accompanied him to a dog show. By the time they left, Gretchen wanted a Dane, too. A Great Dane was of a size and bearing suitable for a Broadway star.

They found the breeder they wanted, but the breeder didn't want to sell a dog of her champion stock to an actress! Eventually, Gretchen and her husband prevailed, and the dog who would become known as Champion Gretchen's Khan of Mountdania went on to make history.

The first stage of Gretchen's transformation from never thinking about pets to being an avowed dog lover began in 1960. She says, "I loved my Danes so much I wouldn't let them go to shows without me. Khan changed my life, he brought out all the mother in me."

Khan was just the beginning. More Danes were to follow. Gretchen Wyler the stage star became a stage mother. She starred in musical comedies, and her dogs starred in dog shows. Gretchen, who has never done anything by halves, was at their side at each of them.

The next stage began in 1966 and transformed Gretchen from dog lover to animal advocate. Gretchen and Shepard lived in Warwick, New York, and Gretchen, by then, was a much-publicized dog fancier. One day she was in a local market when a woman approached her. "Miss Wyler, you're a dog lover, aren't you?" Gretchen acknowledged that she was, and the woman challenged her, "Have you ever been to the dog pound?" Gretchen didn't know Warwick had a pound, but she promised the woman she would go. Her life was about to turn upside down.

In the village dump, behind piles of smoldering garbage, she found a shack that housed dogs and cats in unimaginable conditions. Animals died there of neglect, were euthanized or shipped off to laboratories.

In a total rage, Gretchen called for a town meeting. During the time when she divided her energies between Broadway, London's West End and Warwick, Gretchen managed to establish the Warwick Valley Animal Shelter. Since that time her life has been devoted not only to the dance aspirations of the pretty little girl from Bartlesville, but to the welfare of all animals everywhere. She is, in fact, one of the best-known figures in the humane movement today.

In 1960, when she got her first dog, she also got a horse, a cat and a donkey. It was almost as if she were casting the rest of her life. It started, really, when she and Shepard saw an animal hit by a car. He got out to help it and returned with tears in his eyes. Gretchen says that Shepard's compassion did more than anything else to unlock "it"—that capacity to connect with other creatures—in her.

In 1979, the play *Sly Fox*, in which she starred on Broadway with George C. Scott, brought Gretchen to Los Angeles.

She arrived, she says, "kicking and screaming and promising myself I wouldn't stay." She was certain that she would miss her East Coast life too much, but she did stay and, in time, founded The Ark Trust, Inc. Each year the Ark gives Genesis Awards to individuals in the major media for bringing the plight of animals to public attention, becoming the premier consciousness-raiser in the field, countrywide. The awards ceremony is one of Hollywood's gala events, and it is televised on the Discovery Channel. The thousands of hours Gretchen has devoted to animal issues make that long-ago visit to the pound in Warwick one of the most meaningful side trips ever made by a member of the theatrical community.

At home now in Southern California, Gretchen has four rescued cats and two rescued dogs—a Doberman named Nadia and a Lhasa apso named Mikey. There are two horses, too, Roxanne and Cyrano. They are two of twenty-four Arabians that a breeder was sending off to slaughter. Gretchen learned of the plan and, with a number of Ark Trust supporters, managed to save fourteen of the animals. She placed twelve and kept the two she has now. She has bonded with them as she does with all animals.

Gretchen acknowledges that bonding with a horse is different from bonding with a dog: "A dog is a dependent child. He needs you. I want a horse to dance with me. That's what a horse is, a dancing partner." That's a reasonable perception for a dancing lady from Bartlesville, Oklahoma.

guy coheleach

GUY COHELEACH is undeniably one of the finest American wildlife artists of this century. He has donated millions of dollars to conservation causes through his paintings and prints. But when it comes to the animal world there are really two Guy Coheleachs, not one.

Like the other men and women who do his kind of work, he has spent thousands of hours walking, climbing, looking at and sketching nature, not as many people would like it to be but as it really is. His work has taken him to all continents but Antarctica, and he travels often to Africa. His early enthusiasm for snakes, particularly venomous snakes (his indulgent parents permitted him to keep cobras and rattlesnakes in their basement), expanded into a love for big cats and birds of prey, the subjects for which he is most famous today. They are the wild animals to which he relates best.

All this has made Guy Coheleach at least appear to be tough. He knows nature and understands killing as the means of survival of wild species. It is not a soft and gentle world, and his endless sketchbooks and many of his classic wildlife studies reflect this fact. He stalks his prey like a hunter, then reports what he has seen with enormous precision and truth.

The other side of Guy Coheleach is the big moosh dominated by children and golden retrievers. His wife, Pam, knows that he is a pushover for their kids, grandchildren and his beloved golden retrievers.

Guy's first pets were the snakes he caught and kept from grammar school on. There were other wild creatures, too, for example, a wounded blue jay. In his early years there was a random-bred terrier called Freckles. Like so many dogs most of us remember, Freckles was killed by a car. There was also a German shepherd called Lance who lived for fifteen years.

After Guy and Pam were married there was a little poodle named Snoopy. "She was smart as hell," Guy recalls, "but I never was a poodle man. Not my kind of dog." Golden retrievers are more his kind of dog, and there have been three in a row: Lucky lived to be seventeen; then came Kir, who made it to sixteen; and now there is Mischa, who is only three. "They live pretty well with us. No wonder; we do any damn thing they want us to do. But what a dimension they add to a household," Guy says.

He continues, "Life without a dog would be really empty. I feel good when there is a dog around. If I am away they are an early-warning system, and I feel good knowing that. When I come out of my study, Mischa comes over and checks on me. I would miss that terribly. She is kind of my dog because I'm the one who throws the ball. When I go in and sit down in my chair, pop open a beer and watch a little football, she comes over and puts her chin on my stomach, I just melt. I am a sucker for that. It is so easy to get hopelessly attached.

"You know, I don't think of goldens as animals. I have plenty of animals in my professional life, on safari and here in my studio. Goldens are humans, so help me, they're people. Well, almost.

"I don't see them the way a lot of people do because I sketch them just for the pleasure of studying this incredible three-dimensional object. I sketch my dogs all the time. When you observe the whole animal it is an ever-changing experience. That's what my goldens have been to me, ever-changing experiences. It is like having another family member."

Now the really tough guy speaks: "I love my dogs, I have loved my dogs very deeply. It has torn me apart when the time has come [for them to die]. In my work, I have loved the beauty of the tiger, as I paint them; and the eagles, hawks, owls and falcons, I have loved their incredible beauty. I have been awestruck for much of my life. But that's different. It's not like the love I have had for my dogs."

jennifer heller

JENNIFER HELLER grew up in Westchester, a suburb of New York City, but somehow knew that she didn't belong there. She was meant to be a part of something else. After she finished college in the East she got into her car with her schipperke, Moo-G, and drove to Santa Fe, New Mexico, where she works as a jewelry designer. She has found her place.

"Santa Fe is very supportive of artists. It has a strong sense of community," she says.

Moo-G had a history. He languished in a pet shop for six months, in a wire-bottomed cage. His feet were so covered with scabs that he could barely walk. Jennifer visited him regularly and finally could not stand to see him in pain any longer. Despite her certain knowledge that a pet shop is the last place in the world to purchase a dog, she bought him.

There had been other dogs when Jennifer was growing up; German shepherds, an airedale, but Moo-G was special. He was her rescued friend. He went to her college classes with her, became the mascot of the Sarah Lawrence Equestrian Team and made many friends.

Jennifer and Moo-G arrived in Santa Fe in fine shape and settled into a house with a fenced yard. That part was all-important to Jennifer. She was "hypervigilant" about that gate, but one evening it went unlatched. As far too many dog owners will tell you, that is all it takes, one careless moment and one wheeled vehicle. At the young age of six (schipperkes are normally one of the longest lived of all dogs, readily living twenty or more years), Moo-G perished under the wheels of a car.

Jennifer remembers Moo-G: "Aside from all the clichés about unconditional love and tail wagging when you come home, there is something that animals give that doesn't exist person to person. It is different and extra. I loved giving Moo-G love and care. It was a delicious experience. Animals are not empty or vacant; when you look into their eyes, they look back at you with a conscious knowing. It makes me feel great that a dog can trust me and fall asleep with his head in my lap. That is very special, and clichés just do not address things like that.

"I now have two cats, fish and a new pup, a border collie mix named Sam. If I could, I would have an entire farm! Living without animals is not possible for me. There would be a hole in my life, an emptiness without them. Once, when I lived in an apartment that did not allow pets, I smuggled in some mice."

Jennifer thinks that cruelty to animals should be punished the way comparable crimes against humans are. She is very forceful on this point. Most animal lovers are. It seems to be something upon which all can agree. A pause for a moment's reflection, and then Jennifer continues: "If a person cannot bond with an animal, how can they bond with another human being? All animals want is to love you and be loved."

Indeed. That, after all, is the theme of this book.

anthony shaw

*T*ONY SHAW'S JOURNEY began in the Bedford-Stuyvesant section of Brooklyn forty-one years ago. It has been a long and interesting trip from there. There have been prestigious jobs following a hard-won education. What is notable, from this book's point of view, is that all of it was done in the serene company of a cat, or rather, a series of cats.

Today, Tony is executive vice president and chief administrative officer of the Western Hemisphere's oldest and most admired humane society, the American Society for the Prevention of Cruelty to Animals, the ASPCA. One is forced to conclude that Tony's cats taught him well.

When Tony was ten, his family lived in a house three blocks from a meat-packing plant. One day, a cat walked out onto a loading dock as Tony went by and changed the boy's life. It followed him home. That was Tippy, the first of many pets. Tony has had one or two cats and often a German shepherd ever since.

Tippy and his immediate successors are gone, but now there are Alyss and Miso. Miso is an ASPCA cat. Tony and his wife, Betsy, adopted him at the request of their amazing daughter, Emma Rose (who now has a brother, Gabriel Victor). Betsy came to the ASPCA with Emma Rose to visit her husband. There they met Miso, who was up for adoption. The little girl was just over a year old but she was old enough to conspire. Indeed, a plan was quickly hatched between the women of the family. One evening, shortly after the visit to the ASPCA, when Tony was changing Emma Rose's diaper, the plot was sprung. The precocious little girl looked up at her father and said, "Daddy, I need Miso." Betsy admits that it took her no time at all to teach her daughter that sentence. Tony brought Miso home with him the next day.

Tony reflects, "Not only am I a cat person, I attract cat people into my life. I like the serenity and independence of cats. I swear, when I am with a cat, I can feel my blood pressure go down." Of Miso's unique personality, he says "Miso is a cat who thinks he is a dog. He jumps into my lap and will sit there for hours. Practically everyone who knows Miso tells me that they will take on a cat if it is like him. Even my mother-in-law, who is a dog person, says it. But he is such a moosh I just can't imagine there is another one like him. Miso is the only cat I know who knows how to hug you. He literally does that, as far as his front legs will reach."

Are cat people softer than dog people?

"I think exactly the opposite is true. Cat people, I believe, share a strong sense of self-validation with their companions. Dogs need constant revalidation. Cats know they are superior to people, while dogs tend to settle for a subordinate role.

"Cats bring us to a true sense of self. They force us to reveal ourselves to ourselves as well as to them."

As an example, Tony points out that Alexander the Great, Napoleon and Hitler all despised cats. He explains that "Maniacal overcompensators have to hate cats because in their hearts they lack any semblance of self-confidence."

Tony Shaw may be an overachiever but he is not an overcompensator. He has no reason to fear cats, so he loves them instead. He easily makes room in his heart for them, and they love him back. It would be a terrible thing to feel psychologically threatened by an animal with whom you had tried to create a bond. No chance here. Cats have meant too much to Tony, and he knows and loves them too well for that.

gary larson

GARY LARSON CAN'T REMEMBER a time when he didn't have pets. He recalls, wistfully, "We had pretty open-minded parents." Gary's brother was attracted to pigeons and pheasants, while Gary's choices anticipated his much-beloved *Far Side* cartoons. "Gosh," he says, "I had snakes, lizards, I had a tarantula, tadpoles, a terrarium with frogs and salamanders. Pets may not be the most accurate word, it was more of a mutual tolerance. I've always liked snakes, king snakes are charismatic animals. I had a squirrel monkey when I was in my mid-teens. That was in the bad old days. Pet shops imported just about anything, and people like me couldn't wait to get home with some exotic critter. I even tried raising wasps once. Duh."

But there were more than shelf pets. There were cats: "I'm fond of them but not in the way I am of dogs. I have a tendency to like all dogs, but, with cats, I end up liking only my own."

And, of course, there have been dogs. Starting with his very first pet, a German shepherd mix named Rex, Gary estimates he has had dogs for at least half of the years of his life. Murray—Lord Murray of Windemere, actually—a dark, brindled bullmastiff, is incumbent now.

"Dogs are my brothers," Gary says. "I have always liked them. They are far removed from us as a species, but close because we are both social animals. Sometimes I am outside, wrestling with Murray, and we'll stop and spread out on the grass. I'll use his stomach for a pillow and think how strangely wonderful [our connection] is. It's a powerful bond, amazing, really. I sure don't understand it."

Happily, Gary's wife, Toni Carmichael, is an animal lover, too. Lord Murray has caring, attentive parents and a very nice back yard.

Gary's love of animals has taken diverse forms. At twenty-seven, he worked in an animal shelter. He did that for just over a year and a half. But by the time he was twenty-nine, *The Far Side*, something he had been "fooling around with for a while," started its ascendancy. In its way, *The Far Side* is a celebration of animal life. By the time Gary decided he had "done that enough"—December 31, 1994—the panel was appearing daily in nineteen hundred newspapers. There are over thirty-one million *Far Side* books in print, in seventeen languages. Gary is now deeply immersed with Toni in film projects.

Gary believes that a person's feelings about animals are very important, and very easy to see with Murray around: "You can tell when people come to our house. Some reach out to Murray and connect, and some don't. And vice versa with Murray. A wall is up for some, [there's] instant camaraderie with others. I wonder about people who are on the other side of that wall with Murray; it says a lot to me." Most people probably don't understand that magnificent, muscular Murray is in reality a litmus test. Murray probably doesn't understand it either. Gary does.

As for cruelty to animals, Gary has zero tolerance. He learned much from his time as a shelter worker, and even more through his own kindness toward every living thing. One has only to look at a batch of *Far Side* panels. Although outrageously funny, usually uproariously so, Gary's cartoons show inherent respect for everything from a flea to, well, a human being. The universal appeal of the Larson humor is that he can find great fun in the most mundane things we think and say and do. But it is never mean. He has been known to dip into the well of morbid humor now and then, but when he does he is making fun of it, of negativism and of mean-spiritedness. Gary and his incredible zoo have fun at everyone's expense, even his own.

As for people who are mean to other living things, "It is sociopathic, other-worldly, alien," he says. "I don't believe in the concept of hell, but if I did I would think of it as filled with people who were cruel to animals." As uncharacteristic as it is for Gary Larson to be harsh in his evaluation of others, in this case he means it.

As for Murray, the magnificent, handsome Murray, with jaws that could bend an I-beam, it is the best of all possible lives. Gary, still a young man, has been enormously successful, he is married to a beautiful, caring wife who is his partner, professionally as well as personally. He has his guitar collection and the music that is so important to him. Although his great fame has forced him to retreat somewhat, he lives exactly where he wants to live, exactly as he wants to live. Interestingly, if you ask most people to name the living Americans they would most like to meet, an astonishing number include Gary Larson near the top of the list. With endearing modesty, Gary says of them, "Those people really do need to get out more."

Gary has it all because he also has Murray, and they have the kind of bond he needs. It is hard to think of Gary Larson without thinking of that bond—or of Murray.

phyllis barclay

PHYLLIS BARCLAY, for over fifty years a children's librarian and professional storyteller, was born in Norwood, a suburb of Croydon, England, in 1903. Queen Victoria had been dead less than two years. In about 1909 (Phyllis has an extraordinary memory) the first of her many pets, a smooth-haired fox terrier named Joel, entered her life. As terriers are wont to do, Joel had argued with a local cat and had to go through life with but one eye, but Phyllis recalls that he managed very well.

In time, Joel passed on and a pug named Gyp entered in style. Phyllis's father, Frank Langdon, was a man of taste, given to elaborate gestures in the Edwardian manner, and when the puppy arrived from the family seat in Somersetshire, it was delivered unto Phyllis and her sister Winifred in a basket packed with primroses. The grand entrance seems to have given Gyp a taste for luxury, and he quickly became friendly with a baker named Mrs. Downs who lived down the lane.

Mrs. Downs was ample of person, and Gyp got to be more and more that way as the months passed. Mr. Langdon regularly retrieved him from the alternate residence, where he was employed as a taster by his patroness. When the Langdon family moved to Henley-on-Thames, Gyp, it was decided, would prefer to stay behind, so devoted was he to his work. The comment was made that it wouldn't be long before Gyp exploded.

In 1920, the Langdons came to America and, in time, Phyllis married James Barclay of New York. Their first dog in America, a large and flamboyant Boston terrier named Bonzo, remains her all-time favorite, so she claims.

"Of course, he never really was a dog, he was a person," she says. "He knew that. He truly did. He lived to be eighteen."

Pixie, another Boston terrier and a princess if there ever was one, followed, and so the years rolled on. Phyllis's love of books led her to her half-century career as a librarian. During these decades there were more pugs and a wonderful random-bred dog named Nel. Today there is Sam, an assertive and endlessly loyal Yorkshire terrier much given to recreational barking.

Phyllis notes that "Sam has learned to live with an elderly person. Dogs do learn to live in the style of their owners. He is very set in his ways. If I stay up past eleven o'clock, Sam fidgets and fusses until I go to bed. I put out the light and I hear him take a last drink of water and then he is done until morning. He always wants to be near me and I should be lost without him. I talk to him, really, as if he were a person."

Phyllis adamantly believes in the benefits of pet ownership for older people. She resents clauses in leases and the bureaucratic regulations that deny people the right to have companion animals: "Denying people pets makes a bleak situation very much bleaker. Loneliness is a terrible, terrible situation. An animal becomes a friend and you have to care for it. You have responsibility. An animal can fill a tremendous hole in your life. Everybody wants to be needed. When you are not needed anymore you're through, you're finished.

"Sam needs a lot of love from me. He is very sensitive and if he hears the word 'bad' it upsets him dreadfully, but he thrives on admiration and attention. He fills many, many quiet and potentially lonely moments. I do love Sam dearly."

Phyllis admits that Sam is a favorite dog, too, not just Bonzo: "You can't avoid favorites. You just naturally single some out. They have such strong, distinct personalities."

Phyllis is an expert on the subject of bonding and companionship not only with animals, but with husband, children, grandchildren and great-grandchildren (she has four of the last mentioned). She has had almost all of the twentieth century to study the matter carefully, up close and firsthand.

john castle

JOHN CASTLE has a remarkable relationship with a horse called Spot. Their story is one of compassion and commitment on one side and almost unbelievable understanding and cooperation on the other.

Spot is one of eight horses that John owns, some of which raced for a while, some of which have been used as show hunters and all of which lead the good life when their work is done. But Spot is special.

"He has been telling me for years his name should be Spots," John says. "He is, after all, an Appaloosa. He is the smartest horse I have ever known, just as smart as he can be. He's about twenty-two now, I guess. They said he was ten when I bought him, but there may have been a little Kentucky windage there.

"I put him into the Pegasus Program in Connecticut, where horses are used by the handicapped. It does wonders for people who are challenged—to be able to ride. Spot has always had an enormous sense of who is on his back, whether it is a blind person, a handicapped child, or a very small person. He was always able and willing to adjust his ride to his rider."

But then Spot foundered. The inside of his front hoofs—an area called the frog—dropped, leaving him a cripple. Founder can be caused by trauma, a head injury that draws blood away from the hoofs, by a metabolic accident or by a pituitary deficiency that can come on with age. Almost inevitably horses that founder are destroyed. Most people look on it as a fatal condition. Not so John Castle.

Spot was ministered to by the veterinarians at the New Bolton Center, part of the University of Pennsylvania's superb School of Veterinary Medicine. If a horse can be successfully treated for any disease, condition or accident it will be at New Bolton, where the technology is the most advanced in the world.

"Jim Orsini, Spot's veterinarian, is a genius," John says. "He has probably gone further with Spot than they have ever gone with any horse in his condition. Spot wears permanent fittings on his two front feet, hard silicon foam casts that are precisely fitted. They are replaced every month. The combination of those prostheses, surgery and very aggressive medication has kept him alive—really, it is the enormous amount of care he has gotten from the staff at New Bolton that has kept him

going. About 80 percent of his life is of really good quality, and as long as that is true we'll keep on going, we'll stay with him.

"The advances they have made in Spot's care at New Bolton Center will unquestionably help horses and ponies in the future. They are pushing the limits of technology with Spot, but I feel a great deal of responsibility because of what he did for all those people in the Pegasus Program. He did so much for human beings I feel we should do as much as possible for him." John continues with a smile, "The two of us have developed a very special relationship. When I go to be with him and he lies down, he enjoys having me sit next to him in his stall."

Spot spends his summers in Bedford, New York, and his winters at the Palm Beach Polo Club in Wellington, Florida. When Spot needs his doctor, James Orsini flies to Florida or New York to see him.

Does John Castle love Spot?

"There are multiple reasons for what I am doing. I love this beast, I don't call him a horse, he is a beast, and I do love him. He made a very special commitment to people when he worked in the Pegasus Program and he is so extraordinarily intelligent. We all have fantastic communication with him, and I do not feel that putting him down is the answer as long as a substantial part of his life is of good quality. And many other horses will benefit [from what is learned in caring for him]. In the meantime he has an amazing relationship with the people who render him care. He is affectionate, he nuzzles them, he understands what they are trying to do for him. This horse has had an attitude that has permitted the work that has been done to save him from the usual fate of a horse in his condition. Really, it has taken an incredible amount of cooperation on his part. And, yes, I do love him."

misha dichter

WHETHER HE IS PERFORMING some of the most glorious music ever written, gloriously, or jogging, enthusiastically, Misha Dichter is definitely a *right now* person. That is where English springer spaniel Mercedes, or Merce as she is known to her friends, comes in. Merce is a *right now* dog. If concert pianist Misha Dichter gets the urge to go jogging in nearby Central Park at seven o'clock in the morning, sons Alexander and Gabriel are more likely than not to roll over and groan "Later, Dad," and wife Cipa doesn't want to know. But even at eleven and a half years old, Merce is for the game.

Misha was born in Shanghai, but from the age of two he was raised in California. When he was eight he got his first dog, a random-bred named Champ. Champ lived to be almost fifteen, but by that time the musical prodigy was at Juilliard in New York City. Then the concert tours began. In 1985, settled and married with two sons, Misha got his second dog, and Mercedes took possession of his heart.

Cipa had never had a dog and didn't know what to expect. Imagining the equivalent of another child, she was dreading all the planning that she was sure was going to be necessary—trips to the playground and other entertainments. But Cipa had a weak point. She wanted a country home, and Misha made a deal. They would get the dog he wanted and she would get the house she wanted. Now, with twenty acres, a pool and tennis court, all the Dichters are happy. Cipa has turned out to love Mercedes; athletic Misha has his outdoor arena in which to let off the pressure of the child prodigy turned man, concert star, husband and father; and Mercedes comes alive in the country, loves to swim and shag tennis balls. The whole deal is fine with the boys, now men themselves.

And what is Mercedes, the rather laid back English springer, to Misha Dichter, the *right now*, athletic concert artist? Misha expresses it very simply, "The moment before I walk out on stage to perform—and that is the loneliest moment for any performer—if I can remind myself to think of Merce, as I often do, it has a calming effect." Merce is, Misha says, "everything that is positive, everything that is good and healthy." Those would seem to be assignments enough for any pet.

Misha smiles when he relates that early in the morning, when he usually gets up, if Cipa hears "Hi Sweetie, good morning" in happy musical tones, she knows

it is for Merce. One suspects it is some kind of family joke. Misha says that he and Mercedes hug often and that he talks to her all the time. He doesn't seem to mind that Merce appears to be indifferent to his music. Fortunately, the rest of the world is anything but indifferent.

Any bad experiences for Merce and Misha? Mercedes is an in-close kind of dog. Off lead in the city she stays next to her master. In the country she is seldom more than twenty feet from the house. What she likes to do, she likes to do with Misha. One day Misha was walking with Mercedes in Central Park. She was off lead and by his side, at heel like a perfect lady, but Misha was stopped by the police. "I couldn't believe it," he says with appropriate indignation. "There were drug dealers all around, drugs being bought and sold, and I got a summons for the leash law."

The aesthetic and emotional attractions different kinds of pets, even different breeds of dogs, have for people are mysterious and fascinating. With 157 breeds and varieties of dogs recognized by the American Kennel Club, and with a literally infinite selection of random-bred dogs, why does the English springer spaniel appeal most to Misha Dichter? He says he will always have a springer, listing size as a factor—perfect for the dual life of apartment and country estate. He likes their sporting aspect, too, the jogging and chasing tennis balls. They travel well, are easy in the car, Misha notes, and they are somewhat laid back and not overwhelming. Mercedes was that way even as a puppy.

Does being a good traveler, a skilled tennis-ball retriever, a convenient size for automobile travel explain the deep, personal attachment between Mercedes and the intense concert artist? Probably not. Surely less practical factors are involved. While Misha Dichter appears to have found effective release from the intensity of his profession in his athletic pursuits, his sense of humor and perhaps the odd poker game, he still needs the special benefits of the quiet nonjudgmental friendship of an English springer spaniel. For as long as she is able, Mercedes will continue in her role on assignment to a loving musical wonder named Misha Dichter.

tippi hedren

MOST EXCEPTIONALLY BEAUTIFUL people, especially when they are movie stars, are to some degree unconventional. But compared to Tippi Hedren the other stars in the firmament called Hollywood are about as far out as bread pudding. In Tippi's case, love for animals comes in industrial strength.

She recently listed the animals who make up her immediate family now. The numbers have varied over the years, as is the case with anyone's pet population, but at the moment, Tippi lives on her Shambala Preserve in California with (in varying degrees of intimacy): 24 lions, 11 tigers, 11 cougars, 10 leopards (spotted and black), 4 servals, 1 cheetah, 2 snow leopards, 2 jungle cats, 1 boa constrictor, 3 pythons, 2 house cats, 2 elephants, *many* ducks and 9 human beings. Actually, that is down a little; she once had 150 big cats.

Although no one could quite foresee the magnitude it would achieve when Tippi was growing up in and near Minneapolis, she was always an animal lover. And like all animal lovers she has died a little with each passing pet: "You know they are going to grow old and leave you, but that doesn't make it any easier."

Sometimes they come back in strange ways: "They come to me in my dreams," says Tippi. "I had a lion named Boomer. He thought it was funny to jump on people and bowl them over. He never hurt anyone, he was just playing games. He had a wonderful sense of humor. After he died I had a dream about him, I dreamt that Boomer and I were going to London. He was standing upright, wearing a double-breasted camel's hair polo coat. He was wearing a bowler hat, a cane over one arm. My arm was through his other arm as we boarded the airplane." You wait for more as Tippi tells the story, but there isn't any. That's it.

But a dream of an animal as the perfect regal companion is telling. Growing up, Tippi was so spectacularly beautiful that modeling and then stardom were almost inevitable. Hitchcock discovered her, and with *The Birds* and *Marnie*, she became part of the Hollywood legend. There were other films and TV, of course, and marriage and a daughter (actress Melanie Griffith, Mrs. Antonio Banderas) but Tippi says without apparent regrets, "I am married to the animals, so I have more or less given up a personal life. I don't think of it as a sacrifice [I had asked her if it was]. I would probably die without them. They have taught me so much, added so much to the quality of my life."

Why does she do it? Because they need her even as she needs them. The animals at her preserve are rescues. "I am their last resort. We don't buy, we don't breed. We won't sell them or trade them. Once they come to Shambala they are home. And that is for the rest of their lives. They won't ever have to get into a box or shipping crate again." She is very determined when she says that. Clearly she means it.

Two elephants are among her rescues, Kura, an African cow who had been abused in a circus, and her big African bull, thirty-eight-year-old Timbo. The huge male came to her in 1973 from an animal park near Vancouver, British Columbia. He was "surplus." He would have gone to some half-baked traveling circus-cum-sideshow if Tippi hadn't been there to step in. Tippi was there. And now, she says, "He's my friend—he is an adult friend. You kootchy-coo cats, but an elephant, you talk to him like a friend, you tell him stories. And somehow I am sure he understands."

Strange pets like elephants can have outrageous habits: "At the sight or scent of Clorets chewing gum they go into a state of Nirvana," Tippi says. "They flutter their eyelashes, they look so silly standing there sucking on Clorets. It's not a cheap habit! When they get a pack, they eat the boxes, too." But even a Clorets habit can't diminish the nobility of these magnificent animals. Tippi reflects, "When they come at me through the brush or out of the water, well, it's a great honor. It's like seeing a friend you really love. I often wonder what they think about us. But it is an honor that they let us love them, at least I feel that way."

From Hitchcock to quality time with lions, tigers and elephants in her back yard, it has been a strange but love-filled trip for Tippi Hedren. And she is doing exactly what she wants to do. I am not sure if bonding comes in sizes, but if it does, being bonded to an African elephant must be about as big as it gets.

richard kiley

*T*HE FIRST PET RICHARD KILEY remembers was a smooth-haired fox terrier named Duke. That was when he was a boy growing up on the south side of Chicago. Duke was to be the first of a long string of dogs, but the affair—and it was that, an affair of the heart—ended tragically.

It is a sad story, and as Richard tells it, it is even more touching. His sense of drama, his sense of himself and his very rich voice make it seem as if we are witnessing it ourselves.

"My uncle had a fruit farm in Michigan, and Duke and I went there summers. One day, when I was eleven, I was riding on the tailgate of a truck being driven by a hired hand, a tough kid about eighteen years old. I looked up and there was Duke, tearing down the highway after us. I yelled for him to go back, but he kept coming. He wouldn't listen. I kept yelling, but it didn't do any good. A big black car hit him. The driver kept on going, he didn't stop. Duke was killed, and I watched it happen. I jumped off the tailgate and ran back, crying. I remember it as if it were yesterday. I crouched down over him, but he was dead. I really was crying uncontrollably. That kid who was driving the truck, the real tough one, he had pulled off the road and was standing over me, crying too. He finally pulled me away. Cars were roaring past us. He got me over to the side of the road. We both stood there sobbing."

At about that time Richard was given a .22 rifle as a gift. On his uncle's farm he shot everything—birds, squirrels, anything that moved. One day he shot a squirrel out of a tree. It lay on the ground, not quite dead, its back broken. It was writhing as Richard watched in horror. He never fired the rifle again.

"That was over half a century ago," Richard says. "Even today it puzzles me, I can't imagine how I ever hurt any creature. I could never do it again, and it was a turning point for me." He explains: "I believe very much in the spiritual evolution of our intellect. We've been slow in terms of our sense of compassion. We're still in the cave to some degree—still savages. But we can get there, that's the way evolution works, little doors open in our minds. That squirrel opened one for me, I can tell you."

Richard has had about twenty dogs in his life. His wife, Patricia, is an animal lover, too, but for her, it's cats. She is down to a mere four at the moment. Most of the Kiley pets have been rescue cases, generally street dogs and cats. All but two of

the twenty dogs are random bred. Patricia found one of her kittens cowering on the white stripe in the middle of a major highway, with trucks whizzing past in both directions. She walked out and stopped a whole convoy of eighteen-wheelers to get the kitten, which was within moments of being crushed. That cat lived with the Kileys for twelve years.

While starring in *Man of La Mancha* during its Boston run, Richard found Joey, a Boston terrier, in an alley and brought him home. Patricia found Sun Dance in a woodchuck hole. Meggie, the one surviving Kiley dog, was found cowering under a bush when Richard was out walking the late Joey.

While serving in the navy as a young man, Richard tried to decide what he wanted from life. He knew he wanted a stage career, he wanted to hear applause, he needed it, and he wanted money enough for comfort. He visualized himself as having achieved all of that, and then walking in the countryside with his dog on a beautiful spring day. That was the essence of what he wanted for himself, the way he saw himself. He remembers that vision often, now, as he walks with Meggie near his upstate New York home.

Richard's life is, and has always been, wonderfully full. Along with wife Patricia, there are six kids, twelve grandchildren and even a great-grandchild. Patricia's mother, now a hundred years old, lives with them. There is Meggie and there are the cats.

"Meggie reads me. After nine years, I think I'm learning to read her, too," Richard says. "Animals relate to us on a level totally unknown to us. There is a purity to the love we get from our animals that is truly humbling. Our bonding is extraordinary. When I have to be away on location, Meggie broods. Poor Meggie. There is that wonderful thing between us."

Richard has heard the applause he wanted, decades of it. He achieved all of his goals, in fact, and ponders on the concept of success. "I go back to that vision I had of myself when I was a kid in the navy, the long walks in the country with my dog—that's Meggie now, of course. The stage and the applause are downstate in New York City, the money is in the bank, but aside from family, what success really boils down to is the part with your dog, your truly bonded friend."

marc kalech

ORN IN THE BRONX, New York, Marc Kalech grew up without owning a pet, formally at least. Like a lot of urban apartment kids, Marc compensated. As a ten-year-old, he formed a kind of explorers' club with some similarly inclined neighborhood friends, and together they scouted and hunted over every plot of grass and parkland they could find. The pickings were far richer than their adult neighbors probably imagined.

In Van Cortlandt Park, Marc caught a tiny snapping turtle. He kept it for three years. It lived on chopped meat, doubled its size—to about three inches in diameter—until somehow Marc managed to get it up to the Catskills for release in a lake. He says of it fondly, "It was a wonderful little snapping turtle. I never named it. I just took care of it."

Other finds included occasional pigeons, usually injured, salamanders and the like, and lots and lots of garter snakes. They gave the explorers a great deal to wonder about, and there was actually a place to which they could take their treasures. The monumental American Museum of Natural History opened its arms in a way most New Yorkers probably never knew. There was a room there, albeit quite a small one, where a living collection of New York City wildlife was maintained. Marc and his friends could go to this room and turn in the snakes and things they had found and kept for a while. One assumes that most of the collection was released back into the city's parks and surroundings, but it gave the kids a place to take their finds. They didn't harm nature, they just borrowed from it as from a library.

Equally as unofficial a pet as the creatures he found as an explorer was the little random-bred dog Marc shared with his fraternity brothers while attending college at the University of Miami. Even though he took it home over the summers and south for the school year each fall, it was not really Marc's own special dog. In fact, he has never had a dog.

After graduation, Marc was lonely, living by himself. He decided on a remedy that would give him his first official pet. He adopted a gray striped cat from Bide-A-Wee, a New York–based animal adoption service. He named it Putta-Puttah—according to Marc's mother, the first words he ever spoke. She recalls that it became his childhood name for every cat he ever saw. That Marc's first word was "cat" (after

a fashion) would prove to be prophetic, for since Putta-Puttah, he has rarely been without one.

Anyone who has ever been to the movies knows that managing editors of big city newspapers are tough guys who wear their hats indoors, curse, drink heavily and smoke cigars incessantly. They all look like Pat O'Brien. When you hear Marc talking about Putta-Puttah, it is clear that that image is a fiction. "He was the sweetest animal that ever lived." And live he did, for fourteen years, and Marc Kalech loved him.

Explaining the germ of truth in the stereotype, Marc says, "Journalists do get insulated from human tragedy; they have to in order to survive. I have stopped reacting to it—I've really had to. I've seen a Mafia boss get his brains blown out. I have seen people jump from high places, I have seen more bodies than I can count. The only time I ever lost it was at the site of one shooting. A little white dog had been shot in the eye by a burglar who had also shot its master. It was cowering in the corner, really sick from its wound, but when its mistress came into the room, sick as it was, the poor little thing began wagging its tail and ran to greet her. I just stood there and cried. That's the way I am about animals, I always have been and, you know, I feel there is something right about it. I wouldn't change if I could. Why would I want to?"

Marc originally got Putta-Puttah because he was lonely. Now to keep him company he has his demanding people-oriented job as managing editor of the *New York Post*; his wife, Marcia Kramer Kalech, a well-known television journalist; as well as children, Margot, age seven, and Max (for Maxwell), age two. There are plenty of people and plenty of enriching people-related experiences in the big city newsroom every day. Even so, Marc could never be without the unique companionship of pets. Today, he has Morris and Mookie, two cats he and Marcia adopted from the ASPCA.

"Loving animals is uncomplicated love in the purest form," Marc says. "I never tire of watching two wonderful, healthy, happy kittens playing with each other. I can relax and sleep better at night after seeing my cats stretch and unwind. They show me how to do it, and, yes, I do love them."

edward o. wilson

*I*N HIS SOFT, lingering Alabama accent, Edward O. Wilson says, "There are a number of fundamentally different reasons why people are fascinated with animals." A highly honored Harvard professor, winner of two Pulitzer Prizes, member of the Alabama Academy of Honor—the highest recognition his native state has to offer—recipient, in fact, of just about all the awards a naturalist can get, he still relates easily to the "good old boys" back home, geographically and intellectually removed though they are from Cambridge, Massachusetts, where he has lived for decades. *Time* magazine has called him "the pre-eminent biological theorist of the late 20th century," but he knows and speaks of his roots with affection.

Animals have given Ed Wilson much more than they have given most other men and women of his time. He is without contest one of the greatest entomologists of the century, the world's greatest living expert on ants (a myrmecologist), quite possibly the greatest of all time. With incredible technical fastidiousness he has cared for colonies of ants in his laboratory and home, ants he has collected all over the world, over a hundred species of them. He kept the queen of a Florida harvester ant colony alive for twenty years, "far longer than most pets live." A single leafcutter ant queen can produce 150 million offspring in a decade if it lives that long (they often do) and have three to five million descendants alive at any one time.

Ed Wilson says he has "enormous regard for a twenty-year-old ant," he finds such a creature "magical" and views it with "wonder and respect, but not affection." He adds, "One can scarcely form an attachment to an individual ant. They don't have an attachment to me, nor I to them. Their world is too vast, too diffuse for such a relationship. But there is deep regard on my part." He has traveled endlessly around the world in search of their secrets.

Wilson says, "An ant colony is a superorganism of exquisite functional design and complex chemical communication." He has spent more than fifty years seriously researching that almost unfathomable world and has made many important discoveries. He has taken "deep, constant aesthetic pleasure" in his work but he has, he says, "never wept for an ant."

The mysteries of ant life led Ed Wilson down a perilous scientific path to the formulation of his concept of sociobiology that argues that social behavior—even our

own social behavior and misbehavior—has a strong genetic component. Similarly revolutionary was the theory of island biogeography that he developed with the late Robert MacArthur, which provides a basis for our understanding of the world's imperiled ecosystems and the impending crisis over declining biodiversity.

But that is only one of the fundamental ways in which Ed Wilson relates to the animal kingdom, in that, as he puts it, "thrall of discovery, in the thrill of the hunt, realizing the deepest experience of the explorer, the naturalist and professional scientist." Ants have supported Ed Wilson. The grants that have been given to him so that he could continue his work of exploration have been steady and reliable, reflecting his reliability as a scientist honored in his own time. Ants have been his vocation and avocation. Without a doubt Ed Wilson understands ants and has a deep intellectual commitment to them, but there is that lack of emotional attachment; there have been no tears.

Ed Wilson openly admits, however, that the naturalist has wept for a dog. The last one was a Topy, a beloved cocker spaniel who lived for thirteen years, "lived to be with us . . . and then I had to put him down." And before Topy there was a wirehaired fox terrier and a cat. The pattern goes all the way back to his childhood in Alabama. There was a cat then, too, and a pet alligator. They run like a theme through his memories of childhood, both modalities, his pets and his "specimens." For the pets he had deep affection, and for the others, admiration and wonder.

His travel schedule today—required to accommodate his continuing research, his never-ending need for discovery and his lecture schedule—preclude the possibility of another dog at the moment. The creatures that he is engaged with at the moment inhabit two five-year-old colonies of *Atta cephalotes*, Costa Rican leaf-cutter ants, that reside in his office and in the neighboring Harvard Museum of Comparative Zoology.

Edward O. Wilson says that he and his wife of forty years, Renee, were typical pet owners. Their daughter, Cathy, in every respect an animal person, completes the picture. Perhaps he can go back to that some day. In the meantime there are the ants. One suspects they are a given. The ants will always be there, and centuries from now people will read Wilson the way we read Darwin today.

michelle james

MICHELLE JAMES had always had childhood dogs but her first twelve years of marriage to Ed had been dogless. Ed had never had a dog, and Michelle reports that "it took a long time to talk him into it. He was sure the kids wouldn't help care for a pet. He had no experience." His conversion was sudden. As Michelle tells it, "one day, we were on a ski lift in Vail, Colorado, and Kyra—she was eight, then—said 'Daddy, can I get a dog?' Ed surprised us all and said yes. He even took on the job of finding one himself. Interestingly enough, Ed and the dog—her name is Jazmine; it suits her—have the same birthday."

Kyra, now eleven, has asthma, so a poodle, with its silky coat that sheds less than most other breeds, appeared to be the best choice. Ed chose a standard black version of the great poodle line, and as it turns out, Kyra and older brother (by two years) Brent have made it a family thing. They share the responsibilities of feeding and walking their pet.

As for Ed, there can be little doubt that he was a closet dog lover all along, or at least he was harboring that potential. "My husband now really loves Jazmine," Michelle says. "He seems to be surprised by that. I see him talking to her when he thinks they are alone. It's supposed to be their secret. It was his idea to have her sleep in our room. He even invited her to sleep on our bed. I know now there will be others, more poodles. Jazmine is spayed, so Ed will just have to go and buy them."

Michelle is the executive director of the Charles Ives Center for the Arts in Danbury, Connecticut, as well as being a mother and wife. The fact that poodles are clean and accommodating makes life much easier. She says, "I do love Jazmine. She is like having another good friend. I was an only child, but I always had a dog. When I grew up and didn't have that family dog anymore there was a real void. Jazmine has filled that void. The equation is really very simple: I love Jazmine and Jazmine loves me.

"[Having] a dog is very much like having a sibling. My dog was always with me when I was a kid. When I went away to college—our last dog had run away—my mother went out and got a new dog to replace me.

"During the time I was growing up, I adopted four dogs. You can argue with your parents and later with your spouse and your kids, but a dog never argues back. You just can't argue with a dog. A dog never holds a grudge. If you speak harshly to them they may sulk for a minute or two but they bounce right back. There are no regrets, no resentments, no grudges.

"If you can bond with an animal you can understand how human beings work. I believe that. If you are cruel to or neglectful of animals you probably treat people with disrespect. I would be very skeptical of a real friendship with someone who was cruel or harsh to animals. Somehow that is all tied together.

"In kids, pets really build responsibility. When they take on the things that have to be done they learn a lot of important lessons about life."

When the kids are gone, grown out of the nest, what then? Is the time for pets past? Not according to the Jameses. To quote Michelle, Ed, looking way ahead, says that "when the kids are gone, grown up, we will still have dogs. We've made a real believer out of him. We'll probably stay with standard poodles. They're great dogs, really good friends, and they are clean and easy to care for. I like that."

oleg cassini

OLEG CASSINI, world famous as a fashion designer and very well known, too, as an animal lover, is not known for equivocating. As he sees it, so does he say it. On animals, "the world is divided in two. There are those who love animals, they are bonded, capable of bonding, and then there are the others, and the others don't count. Animals have souls, I believe that, and the others miss so much, they can never understand how much they miss. You can't explain it to them."

And does this arbiter of style and beauty know whereof he speaks, about how much animals can mean in a person's life? The present count on his Long Island estate is eighteen dogs, fifteen cats, ten goats, six sheep, one very large sow of about a half a ton, two Vietnamese potbelly pigs, one donkey, two parrots, twenty-two full-size horses and two miniature horses. And, Oleg adds, "there is me; I am one of the animals."

In 1992, Oleg won a raffle and took home the one thing, it would seem, he really didn't need, another animal. Eight-year-old dwarf miniature horse Miracle, barely nineteen inches tall, may be the smallest horse in the world, Oleg says boastfully (and affectionately).

Today, Miracle is one of his favorites and, it seems, aptly named. A gardener plotted with some cohorts and kidnapped Miracle for ransom. He was gone for four days during which time he was kept in a truck without food or water. Happily, he was found, and the gardener got three months. Miracle recovered fully and is frisky and responsive. He is pastured with the two Vietnamese pigs and five goats, plus Tinkerbell, Oleg's other miniature horse. He loves his carrots and other treats and is dearly loved by Oleg.

Oleg believes there is somehow a genetic component in his love for animals and his skill at bonding with them. When he was nine he was put on a horse for the first time and was declared a natural. "It is strange," he says, "I have never had any fear of animals." Oleg served in the United States Army in the cavalry as a horsemanship instructor. He dismounts as seldom as possible.

He is adamant about the way people should treat animals, saying, "I could never trust a person who didn't like animals, I couldn't communicate with them. They are a different kind of person and I don't understand them." A number of his twenty-two horses were rescued when they were past their prime and about to be butchered, and a good percentage of his dogs and cats were rescued from one cruel fate or another. The donkey joined the menagerie when Oleg read his tragic story in newspapers. The animal had been beaten almost to death by some kids out for a little fun, and Oleg just had to take him in. Oleg is still sickened by thoughts of what that "poor, poor donkey experienced." He has no tolerance for people who are cruel or even indifferent to animals and how they fare in this society we have created.

Oleg has so many animals one could wonder if it is possible for him to bond with all of them. "Yes, yes," he says, "but each in a different way, to a different degree. To the ones that live in the house, naturally, I have a closer bond. But I tell stories to all of them; I talk to them, to my parrots all the time. They all become sad when I have to go back to New York—usually for five days [a week]. They are so happy when I come back and we are together. They cry." He explains to them that he has to leave them to work, to support them all. And so he packs Mr. Flinton, a shih tzu, into the car, and he and his office dog leave the Garden of Eden he has created for yet another week.

Oleg Cassini has led a glamorous, high-profile life surrounded by some of the world's most beautiful and glamorous women. (Jackie Kennedy was not the least of them.) But always there, behind the scenes, waiting for him were his dogs, cats, horses and more. They are spun into a strand that has in turn woven its way through Oleg Cassini's life. Not one of the magnificent fabrics he has commanded in his time has had a more glorious thread than this. Miracle, "sweet and beautiful," is just one thread, for Oleg loves them all.

morley safer

ORLEY SAFER GREW UP in Toronto, and as a kid, he always had dogs—usually strays—and cats, too. His parents were animal lovers, and his father kept goats in the back yard. But early in Morley's career there were the mandatory travels of the evolving journalist. There was the period in Europe and then Vietnam. He was on the road much of the time and as a result this avowed dog lover has only been able to have a dog for about one third of his life.

"My father was such an animal lover that at ninety-three, ninety-four he'd go out every day and feed animals that were being neglected," Morley remembers.

Morley wanted his daughter, Sarah, to really work at being a dog owner, so he waited until her tenth birthday before he and his wife, Jane, bought her her first dog. Now, he says, "I can't envision my life without a dog. It is as integral a part of our lives as anything you can think of. I look on a companion animal as a necessary luxury. I am sure the number of people who would own animals if their lifestyle permitted is enormous. I know for certain that I am not alone in this. My daughter, Sarah, lives in a tiny apartment and she has a dog and a cat. She is so solicitous and careful and caring that much of her social life is built around the needs of her animals.

"All the things people say about dogs are true. When I retreated to the country house to write a book, I was alone with Goldie," a much loved golden retriever that lived for thirteen years. "It was like having another person with me. She was company, there was interdependency, affection, I talked to her. She would lay her head on my foot while I worked, and when she got restless, I knew it was time for a break. We'd take a walk together. In a funny way, she set the pace. There was the time for writing, walking, napping—we took our naps together—then back to the office and work, a break, a swim, it was all with Goldie."

How about the almost inevitable clichés?

"That mantra about a dog giving unconditional love is true, but it makes me uncomfortable because it sounds so selfish. It really isn't selfish, though, because the love goes both ways. They are getting unconditional love as well as giving it. I'm probably overstating this, but I think that our love for animals is a measure of ourselves. Some people suggest that if you care about animals you are callous about people. I am

sure the opposite is true. I would wager that people who give to animal shelters are better to other people than the average population."

After Goldie came Dora, another golden retriever, who is now five years old. Morley says, "Jane and I take Dora everywhere with us. When we visit friends they usually tend to be people who are comfortable around animals. She's a bit of a food thief but is otherwise quite well behaved."

For a person who has spent a lifetime probing, observing and reporting on crime, sins against the planet, war, politics, one could expect a measure of cynicism. It is common among journalists. But pets, bonded animals, are the great levelers, they help iron some of the wrinkles out of life. Whatever he has seen, wherever he has been, Morley Safer has had, for the last eighteen years, Goldie and then Dora to come home to. He sums it up perfectly: "Both are constant reminders of the transient nature of work and the permanent verity of love."

jack lemmon

WHEN HE WAS SIX, in Newton, Massachusetts, Jack Lemmon had a Scottie named Kilty. Perhaps not the most imaginatively named dog on the block, nevertheless Kilty established a pattern. For a little over half the intervening years, one of the most durable and beloved of all Hollywood's film stars has had at least one canine companion.

When their daughter Courtney was between four and five years old, Jack's wife, Felicia Farr, suggested it was time they added a dog to the family again. In a gesture typically somewhat larger than life, Jack did not buy Courtney a dog—he bought her two dogs, black standard poodles, brothers, actually, Champion Virgil of Varner and Champion Walter of Varner. In their Beverly Hills home the brothers Varner lived the good life until they were gathered, each in his time, and went on ahead. Incredibly, almost eleven years passed without a Lemmon dog.

Then, a little over a year ago, Jack began getting restless. He began missing the "love and devotion, and the companionship." He says, of having a dog, "It is fun, just that, sheer fun. It is like being with a friend you love and like to be with. Dogs can be funny as hell."

So enter Chloe, a lovely black standard poodle, the repository of many appropriate star qualities. Why a poodle? Jack reckons that once you have found perfection, stay with it. It is rather like the sage advice everybody gives everybody else, if it ain't broke, don't fix it.

"When we look into each other's eyes, she is very human," Jack says. (Jack and Chloe do a lot of that. Felicia does not mind because she is hooked, too, but she knows that Chloe is really Daddy's dog.) "It is like having a child," Jack continues, "but a child with a terrific sense of humor. I got a bike a while ago and fell off it—I really went down hard. Like a pistol shot, Chloe was on me, licking me, then she lay down beside me. She thought it was funny, but she kept looking at me, asking with her eyes if there was some way she could help."

A lot of people do not realize what being a film star entails. There are certainly rewards, but there are also extremely long working days and nights, endless travel and, sometimes, incredible tension. It is one of the most difficult ways there is to earn a living, albeit often a good one. Although he is one of the coolest guys in town and has become a legend for being easy to work with, like everyone else, Jack Lemmon occasionally needs some help, and he knows where to turn: "Chloe goes everywhere with us. She goes to the office with me every day, and when I am shooting she is on the set. I don't know why she isn't spoiled crazy. We had about sixty extras on the set this week, and they all made a fuss over her. She must get petted a hundred times a day. She loves it. Everyone babies her. You know, with that crazy quarantine law I would turn down an offer to shoot a film in England." (Dogs entering the United Kingdom have to go into quarantine for six months. The British authorities have an almost pathological dread of rabies.)

Jack says, "Chloe's demeanor is incredible. She sits beside me all the time, but the minute we are ready to shoot she goes over and lies down near the camera and follows everything I do with those intelligent eyes of hers. Sometimes I think she must be human. She has never messed up a single take yet. Recently I was in a scene and there was a table covered with a cloth. When the director said cut, I saw a little black nose and two paws inching out from under the cloth. She had hidden there without making a sound until we were done with the scene. She wanted to be a little nearer to me."

It is perfectly obvious how Jack feels about Chloe. When she is nearby, when he can look at her and touch her, the tension, even the tension of a movie set, eases and the job to be done is facilitated. Will Chloe the movie-set dog ever have a career of her own? Is that what destiny has prescribed?

Jack responds, "She was in *My Fellow Americans* with Jim Garner and me. She played a lesbian—she marched with a group of gay women in a gay rights parade. She didn't make the final cut, unfortunately. I was chagrined! It can be a tough business, you know."

gail bird

GAIL BIRD and her jewelry-designing partner of twenty years, Yazzie Johnson, provide a kind of oasis of compassion in northern New Mexico. Although they now live with just two dogs and three cats, the resident population has varied frequently. They live in an area where a great many people, unfortunately, neglect to spay or neuter their animals. Abandonment along country roads is an accepted way of dealing with the inevitable result.

Although Gail didn't have a pet until she was eighteen and living in Berkeley, California, she has become over the years the best kind of animal lover there is, caring and responsible.

She says of her pets: "They are not really my family but they are real close to it. I don't think of them as children the way some people do. You can't choose your family, but you can choose your friends and you can choose your animals. I like that. I like my pets an awful lot. Okay, I love them.

"It's terrible what people do. They don't care for their animals. It is really sad. We see a lot of animals dead on the road. We pick up strays all the time and try to find them homes or at least take them to a shelter. We can't keep them all. There is a downside to living in the country. People from the city drive out and dump their pets. We found a whole litter of puppies abandoned in a culvert. They were wild, and we couldn't get to them. We left food for them, but we don't know what happened to them. Things like that happen all the time.

"People here in northern New Mexico have one of the highest poverty rates in the United States. It is not a prosperous area and almost the last thing people around here do is get medical care for themselves. Medical attention for their pets is even further down the list. They just don't do it. They can't."

Gail's and Yazzie's relatives think it's odd that they keep their animals in their house. Even though the Pueblo and Navajo peoples have kept dogs for an extremely long time, they have traditionally been work animals that did not share living space with their owners. Gail and Yazzie's attention to their pets is considered unusual.

Most of Gail's smaller pets are dark in color which camouflages them from the owls, coyotes and packs of wild dogs that can make life hazardous when the sun goes down. Bears come through the area near her home occasionally, and mountain lions do too.

Gail is Santo Domingo Pueblo on her father's side, Laguna on her mother's, Yazzie is Navajo. Gail speaks of a "tradition of respect for everything around us. That is how you are supposed to live." Yazzie and Gail do show their respect in several ways. In the jewelry they make, they use a great variety of materials often overlooked by other artists and they are known for that. The animals they absorb into their lives have also been largely ignored and need their oasis of concern. In a recent magazine article, Gail is quoted as saying: "You make use of what is in your environment, what is precious to you and what you find appealing." She was speaking of the jewelry she and Yazzie design and make, but she could have been talking about her pets.

charles osgood

THE WORLD AND LIFE as it is lived by Charles Osgood are filled with the wonder and excitement of living things. After thirty years as a CBS broadcast journalist, he is one of the best-known and most highly respected members of his profession. Charles and his wife, Jean, have five children, ranging from Jamie, a ninth grader, to Kathleen, a college graduate now living in Boston. In between are Winston, Annie and Emily.

But the family doesn't stop there. The Osgoods traditionally always have two dogs—"the young dog and the old dog"—and right now, that means Cleo, a one-year-old dalmatian, and Tony, a seven-year-old Portuguese water dog. And there are more—two barn cats, Cat #1 and Cat #2, and even rabbits, fish and a parakeet.

The first pet Charles recalls was Inky, "a wonderful little mutt who looked like a small Doberman pinscher," and who was part of the Osgood family between Charles's fifth and fifteenth years. He reflects, "Inky was very much a part of my growing up."

Also early on there was another random-bred dog named Max that Charles will hesitantly acknowledge as his all-time favorite. There was a boxer that wouldn't be housebroken and had to go and live elsewhere. Everett (after Senator Dirksen) and Cecilia, two Old English sheepdogs, are fondly remembered, and there was a beautiful German shepherd called Lady.

"Having two dogs is like having two kids," Charles explains. "There is great competition for attention. Just like interacting with children, you have to be fair; fairness is very important—in going for walks, food, giving treats, any kind of attention. Dogs and kids monitor what you do."

The Osgoods live in an old Victorian house near New York City, and they have a second home in France. There is a couple in residence there, and to them the Osgoods take their second canine family—greyhounds rescued from tracks in the United States. They are flown from life in cramped cages to the French countryside, where "they learn to 'speak' French—respond to commands in French—and live the good life." Charles loves to watch them run as they self-exercise and takes great satisfaction in watching them free and happy.

For all of his involvement with animals, especially dogs, Charles, the master word crafter, is cautious about a word like "love." It is one he takes very seriously. "I think you have to be careful not to confuse love for our pets with the love we express for a spouse or for kids. There is certainly genuine affection for animals—puppy love, literally—but it isn't the same." He continues, "You share your life with your pets. Our dogs sleep in our bedroom. I think they are comforted by being with their human family. I know that I am comforted when I am with them. But that love is not to be confused with human familial love. We are wanting for the language to express the difference."

Charles is a profoundly thoughtful person, and his depth and his intellectual honesty have made him, for three decades, one of the most worthwhile people to listen to in American broadcasting. Reflecting on a book he once read about our relationship to dogs—possibly Konrad Lorenz's *Man Meets Dog*—he says, "I think that the first true genius may have been the person who had the idea to take in a dog or wolf as a companion." And continuing, "I suspect that by now there is some kind of instinctive, primal satisfaction we get from dogs—like our reaction when we sit in front of a blazing fire. Dogs evoke a sympathetic reaction in us that even people can't."

What will happen when all five kids are off living on their own? Charles is sure of the answer: "Oh, we'll always have dogs. That's forever."

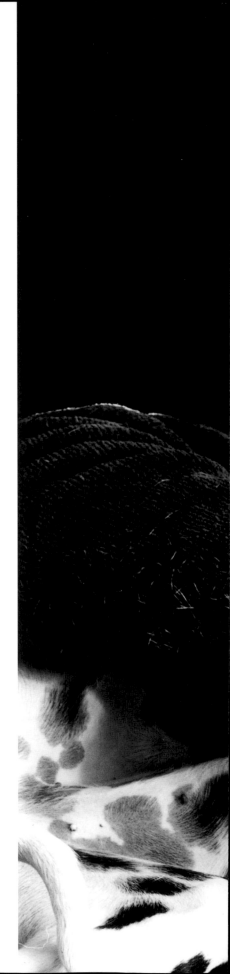

charles lugo

TEN-YEAR-OLD Charles Lugo goes to a very special school in Brewster, New York, called Green Chimneys. This world-famous educational facility operates on the principle that if you bring people in need together with animals, wonderful bonds are formed and all can benefit.

Charles was born in New York City, one of three children. Somehow the mix of kids, home, school and the street was less than ideal for him, and it was decided that another approach to life—one involving animals—was worth a try.

"It took me a while. I didn't know about animals," Charles explains. "I like big animals a lot. I finally picked a sheep with horns 'cause I liked the horns. I began to like the sheep more and more. Now, I am attached to sheep, especially Hazel. I talk to her all the time. Sometimes I talk to her when she pulls hard on the lead and the oxygen comes out, and when I talk to her she feels better.

"If I have a bad day, I go see Hazel and she makes me feel better. I tell Hazel how I feel and she hugs me. I know she can't really do that, but I feel like she does. Animals can help you even though they can't speak. They talk in their own language, and we can understand them."

The fact that a ten-year-old youngster, on a bad day, feels as if he is being embraced by his friend Hazel is really what Green Chimneys is all about. Each child finds the way by first bonding to animals and then bridging those new-found bonding skills to peers and finally to the school's adult faculty and administration. Charles's connection is with Jacob sheep and snakes. He is very fond of a two-foot python called Spot. But above all others, Hazel is his very special friend.

"She might butt other people with her horns," Charles says, "but she would never do that to me. People think she has horns so she must be a ram. She isn't. Jacob sheep females have horns, too, and I like that."

The theme of this book is reflected on Charles's face when you talk with him about Spot and Hazel, mostly Hazel. That theme, after all, is what animals mean to people. His insight is amazing, and you know that the whole learning and loving experience will play an important role in whatever else he does from here on in.

"Before I came here I didn't know much at all about sheep. I didn't know about what animals can do for you. But I do now," he says.

Charles is a bright, animated kid, charming and full of wonder. He appreciates his relationships with animals and seems to understand how he is transformed when he is having a bad day and seeks their company. It seems his encounter with bonding with animals has given him a whole new outlook on life. He says, "My uncle in Puerto Rico has a farm. Maybe, someday, he will give it to me."

One hopes he will.

mary tyler moore

MARY TYLER MOORE'S ASCENT to stardom has been made easier, one has to believe, by her love of animals. It is a deep attachment that is an integral part of her. She seems to derive a kind of energy from the enormous empathy she has for her fellow creatures. She is a vegetarian, and her compassion extends to all animals, but she is foremost a dog person.

"I love all animals, but for everyday living it's the dog. I feel about my dogs now, and all the dogs I had prior to this, the way I feel about children—they are that important to me. When I have lost a dog I have gone into a mourning period that lasted for months," Mary reports.

When Mary was born, in New York City, Wendy, a black cocker spaniel, was waiting. Family lore has it that Wendy slept under Mary's crib, and if Mary cried, Wendy cried right along with her.

When Mary was nine, her family moved to Los Angeles, but Wendy had to remain behind. It was a very difficult time for Mary. Not long after the move, Mary came upon a man beating a dog. She attacked the man furiously, pummeling him with her fists.

"I knew I had to do that—at absolutely any cost—I had to save that dog," she says. In one way or another she has been attacking animal abusers ever since. She is a member of the National Advisory Board of the ASPCA, and she contributes to other humane societies as well. It is just one of the ways she feels she can make a difference. Since, when Mary speaks, Mary is heard (celebrity does have its advantages), it matters very much that she is vocal on the matter of animal abuse. And she is vocal! One seldom has to wonder what concerns Mary Tyler Moore or how she feels about it.

When Mary was ten, she got her second dog, a beagle she called Jeff. One day, when Mary was out in front of her house, her mother drove up and Jeff ran out to greet her. While Mary watched, he was struck and killed by a car. She hasn't really put that memory to rest.

"I am amazed—angered—when I see a dog off its leash," she says. She has seen where that kind of carelessness can and so often does lead.

Today, there are two dogs in Mary's life: Dash, a golden retriever, and Dudley, a petite basset griffon vendeen, an old French breed generally known as the PBGV.

There are also two goats, five horses and "lots and lots of fish, and no one is allowed to catch them." Mary and her husband, cardiologist Robert Levine, have a 123-acre country estate north of New York City, and a stream feeds five ponds on the property. The network is a kind of fish sanctuary. Robert, in his own way, is as much an animal lover as Mary is, with an enormous fondness for wildlife. His admiration for the big cats and other predators is profound.

What if Robert did not share Mary's passion? "It would have been a hungry experience if Robert hadn't been an animal person." But, no worry, Robert went through school with his dog by his side in the classroom.

Before Mary and Robert met, Mary lived alone in New York City without a pet. She reflects, "It was life on a different level." Within six months of their marriage they had Dash, the golden retriever. They used a crate at night as part of the training regimen, and Robert slept on the floor next to the crate for the first couple of nights until the puppy settled in.

On the subject of intelligence in their dogs, Mary, like most dog owners, has an opinion: "Dogs have an intelligence that is different from ours, but it is every bit as important. If only we had found a way to tap into it, how much better off might we be today!"

And you know Mary firmly believes that is so. On the subject of people who are insensitive to animals, does Mary Tyler Moore trust them, could she?

"Absolutely not! I don't trust them. I pity children I see shy away from animals. They would be so much more sensitive when they grew up if they knew how to care, they would understand differences so much better, they would make much better people."

Mary's feelings for animals are passionate and very much a part of who she is. Her own tremendous success as an actress and the adulation she has known for so long are a part of who she is, too. But the animals have always been there, and the love she feels for them, the anger she feels for people who are indifferent or actively hostile to those creatures who reside at the very core of her own life. She fights for what she believes in, and one of the things she believes in is the right of animals not to suffer at the hands of man.

perry knowlton

*F*OR LITERARY AGENT Perry Knowlton, living with animals is the normal way of life, an accepted adjunct to human relationships. From the time he was born in Manhattan there has been a parade of pets, all still remembered with reverence. Peggy Ann, an Irish setter, was first, followed by her thirteen puppies.

Whiskey, a Saint Bernard, came next, and an English cocker spaniel called Ruddah. Then came a floppy-eared Great Dane named Danny. Perry would never be long without the companionship of animals. Throughout his marriage and family life with a son and two daughters (all of whom now work with him at his literary agency), not to mention three grandchildren so far, animals have always been an important part of his life.

When Perry returned from duty with the army in Germany it was in the company of Argos von Schloss Hautzenstein, a splendid German shepherd. Back in civilian life, Perry worked as an editor at Scribner's and lived in Dutch Neck, near Princeton, New Jersey. Rats were a problem, and Perry turned to a natural solution—Anthony, a Siamese cat who arrived on Christmas Eve. When the family Knowlton descended the stairs on Christmas morning, Anthony was sitting at the bottom, waiting for them. Three rats' tails were lined up beside him. Perry has been very fond of cats ever since.

In time, Percy, a yellow Labrador, and Sprite, a cocker spaniel, joined the household. Then Perry's love affair with poodles began with Friday, a standard, and her puppy, Puck, and a much beloved miniature, Honey. Now there is also Night Shift, a cat. A few years ago, Perry tangled with a bad oyster and became seriously ill with hepatitis. To this day he firmly believes that Night Shift and Honey kept him alive through that very bad time.

Perry's most serious animal love affair, however, is of a different sort. It was foretold in the summer of 1937, on his first day at sailing camp in Maine. The campers were having a picnic near a tall seaside conifer that held a giant osprey nest. Perry climbed the tree and peered into the nest. He was bewitched by what he found there. Without considering the consequences (most ten-year-old boys do not worry about consequences), Perry grabbed two chicks and stuffed them under his shirt. It was a different kind of time with different sensitivities.

Although the odds were against him, Perry managed to raise the chicks. He caught fish, pounded them between two rocks and fed his demanding infants. Later

in the summer he wrapped his arms in towels and ran around a field near the camp, flapping his arms as the birds flapped their wings. He taught them to fly. He took his maturing charges to tidal pools where they learned to hunt. By the end of August, they were on their own. In those days, there was a $2.00 bounty on osprey (supposedly to protect fishing interests) but also a law forbidding their removal from the state. Perry let his summer charges go free.

Although it would be over half a century before he was possessed by another bird of prey, the course was set. In the intervening years there would be parrots, including today's talkative Bird Brain, an African gray, but Perry remained fascinated by winged hunters. He longed to be a true falconer.

In 1995, Perry gained the sponsorship of a neighbor, a licensed master falconer, and began his two-year apprenticeship. Now Perry has passed his exams for his state and federal licenses and is both a falconer and a wildlife rehabilitator.

In the thirteenth century, Frederick II, king of Sicily and emperor of the Holy Roman Empire, wrote a 650-page treatise on falconry, which Perry has studied (translated from its original Latin), so it was natural for him to name the first hawk he trapped Frederick III.

"You are not supposed to make pets of them; they shouldn't be spoiled, you should be able to release them back into the wild," Perry says. "But there is a real relationship. If I call to him he will fly to my fist from 150 yards or more. He isn't a pet, he doesn't sleep in my bed like a dog. He is a bird, he is 'manned,' which means he's learned to put up with man and his surroundings, but he is not tame in the usual sense. I certainly like him a lot. I talk to him, he is named, after all, and a lot of falconers don't do that. However, he is very definitely not a companion. Do I love him? Yes, of course, but in a different way, and I can't really explain that. [The falcons'] wildness, which never goes away, is a big part of their appeal. I have dogs, two cats and parrots for animal loving in the conventional sense, but a wild hunter who will work with you and come to you on command is another dimension. In falconing, a beautiful wild bird cooperates with enthusiasm and apparent pleasure with a human animal it, at least partly, considers to be a friend and partner. This is love combined with tremendous admiration and respect."

marvin hamlisch

*M*ARVIN HAMLISCH has another love besides music. It is a slightly random-bred yellow Labrador retriever named Jessye. Marvin is very earnest about this passionate attachment, and Jessye is, too.

Marvin grew up on New York's West Side, and the life his parents led just couldn't accommodate a pet of substance, or at least they were not so inclined. There was, however, Marvin recalls, a parakeet named Snooky.

A lot of time passed, a lot of fame accrued and Marvin had homes in both New York City and in West Hampton on Long Island. About twelve years ago, there was, from Marvin's point of view, a fortuitous set of circumstances. He had just broken up with his girlfriend when a hurricane hit the Hamptons. He felt he should go out and check on his house. Things weren't too bad there, but driving back to the city, with plenty of time to think, he finally admitted to himself how lonely he was. On impulse he swung by an animal adoption agency, the North Shore Animal League.

Sparky, a tiny orange-and-marmalade kitten, was waiting for him, and animals entered Marvin's life. Sparky is today, a dozen years later, still an extremely gregarious, interactive, people-oriented cat.

Great though he was in the role of pal and companion, Sparky wasn't really a cure for the loneliness of bachelorhood. Then Marvin met Terre and the twosome became a threesome.

About two years ago, Marvin and Terre decided to start the search for the perfect Hamlisch dog. Marvin went back to the shelter where he had had such luck with Sparky and promptly fell in love with a little yellow puppy. He brought her home, Terre took one look at the nondescript dog and asked, "Are you kidding? What is that?" She soon found out—Jessye was destined to become what Marvin proudly describes as "the Queen of the Campus."

In no time, Marvin and Terre and their housekeeper, Shirley, found themselves out on Park Avenue with trainer Brian Kilcommons, working to turn Jessye into the most intelligent dog in the world.

"Her eyes are on me, she looks at me, *she listens to me,* she cares about me. It was instant bond," Marvin reports.

"If I am out walking her and someone walks toward me, she growls until I tell her it is all right; then she is fine. Really, she would kill for me. I wish I had known when I was eighteen instead of fifty what I know now. What a way to meet people and make new friends! Just walk a dog. Everybody stops to talk to you. You know, 'Who's your vet? What dog food do you feed her? Where do you take her for exercise? Do you use a groomer?' People really trade information. You look for each other and greet each other when you are out."

When he is on tour, Marvin and Terre leave Jessye with Brian and Sarah Kilcommons. Jessye has learned to play both soccer and ice hockey there "at camp." She is what Marvin calls "your basic sports fanatic." When he is away, Marvin calls in no matter where he is. Not long ago he called Brian from Slovakia to hear how Jessye's soccer game was going. He was told he would have to wait a week before getting her back. She was the best soccer player in the camp, and they needed her for a game. (Her team won. Jessye had a scratched nose, but she was a winner.)

"I love her unconditionally, as she does me," Marvin says. "You know, I lead a pretty stressful life, and she really gives me an opportunity to unwind. I can't believe I waited so long to find her. I should have had her thirty years ago. Terre says she is a better snuggler than I am. I will tell you this, there is no way in this world I would ever again live without a dog. No way!"

You instinctively believe him. And Marvin Hamlisch has a dream: "I am performing onstage. I am coming to the end of a great piece on the piano. Jessye comes onstage wearing her little tuxedo. And she comes up right at the end and plays the last note just as I have trained her to do."

Is that possible?

"We're working on it, we're working on it."

carol burnett

FOR THE FIRST TIME EVER, Carol Burnett has her very own cat. There were cats and dogs when her children were growing up but somehow that was different, she says. Roxy is hers and hers alone, and they are a bonded pair, off to see the world as a team.

It happened in New York when Carol was starring on Broadway in *Moon Over Buffalo*. She was living in a hotel and one day just decided she needed a critter. There were a lot of cat people in the cast, and they went to work on her the moment she let her thoughts be known—and cat people can be a relentless lot. A cat would be easy to care for. It could come to the theater with her. She wouldn't have to walk it. It could ride in a carrier. It wouldn't bark and make a lot of noise. It would offer great companionship. It would purr. It would snuggle. When she left the show her cat could travel with her. Carol was convinced.

One day, Carol went to a local animal shelter called Bide-A-Wee and asked for advice on how to select a cat. The cat, she was told (*"pardon me!"*), would select her. So, with some trepidation, "I began walking up and down the aisle in front of the cages waiting for something—for 'it' to happen, and it did. A little paw came out and I heard a meow and that was it. They took us to the Get Acquainted Room—don't you love it?—and Roxy went on to become a theatrical cat, the mascot of the show.

"She has a lot of Maine coon cat in her, I am told. She has a great personality, she is just terrific with people. She was only eleven weeks old when I got her, and everybody in the cast handled her every night. She really is gregarious, very well socialized. I always thought I was a dog person, but now that I have Roxy in my life, I don't know. She responds to verbal commands. I went out and got some cat books and studied them. As long as you are consistent they really do learn the lifestyle you want them to live with you.

"I travel so much, constantly, traveling everywhere, jumping around. She's so easy, she's great under the seat, no trouble, you wouldn't even know she is there. I do have an argument with her about getting into her carrier, but I always win."

Life does have its little glitches. Carol pays a price for the friendship she has with Roxy: "I am allergic to her, but I am keeping her. I would rather get rid of my

allergist than Roxy. I'm not about to give her up. I'll take the shots if I have to, but Roxy stays."

There is an inevitable question when talking about cats with one of the most outrageously funny people who has ever lived—do cats have a sense of humor?

"I really don't know. But cats make me laugh and maybe that's the same thing. They do such crazy things. Roxy has me laughing all the time." She gives an example: "Last July, I was rehearsing for a show for the Hollywood Bowl. We were working here in the living room with the music people. Now, I have a very loud voice, very! Like Ethel Merman. I hit a really loud note, I really let go, and at first Roxy simply tapped me on the shoulder. Then I hit the big one, you know, the *big one*, really loud, so she slapped me in the face. No claws but a real slap as if she were telling me to snap out of it. We nearly fell down it was so funny. She slapped me for making too much noise!

"I see Roxy as a soul. There is something there. It isn't a human soul, it's a cat's soul, and she deserves that, having her own kind of soul, whatever it is. There is real communication with her, it's the natural order of things. It's unconditional communication in an unconditional relationship, and that's good."

Will there be more animals?

"I don't know. I travel so much, and Roxy doesn't know she is an animal. I don't think I could travel with more than one and, besides, as long as she isn't around other animals we have this secret about her identity. She is so very comfortable with people."

Okay, Carol. We won't tell Roxy she isn't people if you don't.

karen dorn

KAREN DORN, farm manager and volunteer wildlife rehabilitator, has been an all-out animal lover all of her life. It's an extra, special dimension. Her parents were similarly afflicted, and she has memories from early childhood of a raccoon being nursed back to health. At one point, there were twenty or so turtles in the family, she recalls.

Today, with the help of Tacker, her husband of nineteen years, and their three teenagers, Karen is keeping the faith. She has (deep breath required) one alpaca, one sheep, two barn cats, one house cat, two dogs, one conure, one goat, two horses, four rabbits, two guinea pigs, one chinchilla, two pythons and a tank full of fish—no head count available. It is the Dorns' way of life.

Her work as a volunteer wildlife rehabilitator for mammals means that in the spring there are usually a couple of the feed-every-two-hour-type visitors that have been orphaned or hit by cars. There is always somebody waiting to be fed in the Dorn household, and Karen loves it because she has so much love to give.

"Really, they give me a high. Nothing about animals intimidates me, no matter how big they are. They make me feel needed. I like that. They amaze me every time I think about them," she says.

"My only regret is that their lives are so short. That is hard. But I would be empty, my life would be totally empty without them, even though I love my husband and adore my kids. I need them, too, the animals.

"It's a different kind of love. What you get from animals is altogether different. It's hard to explain. It's just something you feel. My animals never get mad at me no matter what goes wrong. It makes me feel good inside knowing that is waiting for me when I get home. All they want is a kind word and a pat on the head. And look what you get back!"

And how would it have been if Tacker hadn't turned out to be an animal lover too?

"It took Tacker a while to get used to the numbers of animals, but he did it. He understood what it meant to me, and now I know our lives are better for the animals we have and the care we give them."

It is not always a peaceful life, or an easy one, being an extreme animal lover like Karen. She reflects, "There is something in my head I can't control—I don't think I want to—when I see an animal in trouble. It is as if it were a child calling for help. I have to act, I have to rescue it and stop its pain. Its suffering goes right to my heart, I feel it so deeply." This undeniable impulse has gotten Karen in trouble. She has had guns pointed at her, she has been threatened with calls to the police and possible court action, all because she saw an animal in trouble and acted the only way she can act.

"Animals have so much to teach us about love," she says. "Our kids learn from them, they learn about love and caring and responsibility. It is such a wonderful experience when you are bonded. I wanted my children to experience that, and now they have.

"Every animal has so much to offer that is unique. Every animal is different, [offers] a different kind of bond. Even rabbits: they are so soft and gentle and innocent. With dogs it is their great devotion—you just can't do anything wrong in their eyes.

"If I died tomorrow, I would die happy. I have been so blessed by my family and the animals in my life."

For those who claim that loving animals is a sure sign of misanthropy, Karen is the perfect living argument in opposition. Very happily married to a fine, strong husband, an extremely attentive mother to three loving teenage children, and with a wide circle of friends, she is yet bonded to virtually all the animals she encounters. A jet black alpaca named Heidi can testify to that.

joe garagiola

FOR JOE GARAGIOLA, professional big league ballplayer, radio and television personality, loving dogs came about by way of a conversion. When he was a kid growing up in St. Louis, Joe's family didn't have a dog, but their neighbors did. The two families were as close as relatives, and that made it all the harder when the Berra dog (not Yogi's family) bit the Garagiola kid, badly. Understandably, Joe took it personally. He swore that he would "never, never, never have a dog." He stuck by that position for years.

Even his family, wife Audrie (of forty-seven years now) and their three kids couldn't convince him. (Today, Joe Jr. is general manager of the newly franchised ball club, the Arizona Diamondbacks; Steve is a television sportscaster in Detroit; and Gina is a writer—and there are now eight grandchildren.) The big change came when Joe was broadcasting the Yankee games. He had a good friend, a theatrical agent named Joe Glaser, who was a big-time dog man. He bred and showed toy poodles and made it his goal to get Joe Garagiola hooked. Joe wasn't buying into the idea. He was still intent on never having a dog.

But things in life happen in strange ways. Gina, then six years old, had to undergo very painful medical tests. Although the episode would have a happy ending, the tests, Joe was warned by the doctors, would be grueling. In an effort to bolster his daughter's courage, Joe told her if she would be brave he would buy her anything in the world she wanted. Gina answered, pre-dictably, "Daddy, I want a dog." Joe Garagiola called Joe Glaser, and the course was set.

From that day until very recently, the Garagiolas have always had two dogs, tiny dogs, toy poodles or Yorkies. Sassy, their most recent dog, died not long ago, and Joe and Audrie were devastated. Joe says, "When you have to take a dog on her last ride, it is terrible, terrible. I guess you don't really own a dog, you rent them, and you have to be thankful that you had a long lease. You are bonded, hooked."

As for dogs liking you: "You really have to be some kind of a creep for a dog to reject you."

Joe was hooked from the start, although it took him a few days to realize what had happened in his life. He recalls, "Those first dogs, toy poodles—we called them Wellington, or Welly, and Napoleon, or Nappy—seemed to know I was antsy. They were out to prove me wrong. They seemed to say, 'You have to like us,' and they were right."

Joe adds, "All a dog wants is a chance to love you. In baseball, you think you own the ball but in reality the ball owns you. It's the same thing with dogs. You just think you own a dog. The dog owns you and they know it. They know everything. I don't care what you do, your dog is a part of it, and if you don't know it, they do—they have it all figured out."

Sassy and Sweetie, the two Yorkies, were the last dogs owned by Joe and Audrie, but they are on the brink of getting others. At the moment they are baby-sitting Gina's bichon frise, Cookie.

Joe is now part of the team that announces and provides color for America's premier dog show, the Westminster Kennel Club Dog Show in Madison Square Garden every February, and he is frequently challenged with barbs like, "Hey, Joe, why don't you get a real dog." He shrugs, "I've never had a big dog. I'm a little-dog guy. I want to be able to hold my dog. I'm secure, I don't have to prove anything, I don't need an image builder. All I want to do is love."

For Joe Garagiola it has been a long trip, 180 degrees, from dedicated non-dog owner to this: "For me, all I need to know about dogs is that I love them, and dogs seem to say to me, 'Okay, you can love me.' That's it, all of it."

Yup, Joe Garagiola is secure, in more ways than one.

anne graul

ANNE GRAUL INSISTS that she can remember the day she got her first pet. He was a black cocker spaniel named Acey. It was Christmas morning, and Acey was sitting in a rocking chair with a red ribbon around his neck. What makes the story amazing is that her memory is crystal clear although Anne was only a year old at the time.

With and after Acey came an indeterminate number of cats, a black-and-white cocker, a Chesapeake Bay retriever, ponies, burros. She smiles. "Anything that had fur on it, I wanted, I begged for, and when I was big enough I brought it home under my arm and hid it in my room."

Her animal-loving parents indulged her passion, and her husband, Tom, another marked animal lover, obviously does, too. The present count is six dogs, eleven cats, twelve horses, ten peacocks and around thirty-four bantam chickens. "Mean old Mr. Fox does cause that number to vary from time to time," Anne says.

"I've never been without animals, ever. They are my whole life. [Not quite true. Anne is happily married and has an extremely active social schedule. She and Tom travel a great deal.] They are my way of life, they are my work, my hobby. I can't imagine life without them.

"I know people who don't have animals, and I wonder what they do. If you have a bad day—everybody does—and you come home and just hold a pet, you can feel the tension bleed away. I don't have any friends who don't have animals. I just don't trust people like that. There is something wrong there, something is missing."

Asked if she has favorites, she at first denies it, then smiles warmly and admits that she does. "My horse, Roger. He is the greatest horse in the world, and I love him. He and I can do anything together. My favorite dog? All of them. I have taken in a lot of abused animals. That's what I do, that is my life. Whether horses—people abuse horses more than any other animal—or dogs, my heart goes out to all of them.

"Tommy loves our animals, too, only he might prefer it if we didn't have quite as many as we do now. I go get them, and in the end he loves them as much as I do. Thank God he is so nice about it. He was raised with lots of animals like I was. It would be awful if one spouse didn't like animals. I couldn't stand it—I would just wave good-bye. Adios. I would have to."

Not all of the Graul animals are anonymous orphans of the storm. One of their twelve horses is Sword of Alydar, the great Alydar's son. He originally sold for $2,000,000, but his owner and his trainers all gave up on him. He was considered a rogue, and he really did hurt people. "They practically gave him to us just to get rid of him," says Anne. "They were thinking of killing him, he was that dangerous. Now, he and I are great friends. He can be a little tricky, but he is gentle with me. I have his trust. The story is that he had been abused. He just didn't trust anyone; he had learned not to. It is such a sense of achievement to get inside of an abused animal and earn its trust. You can turn them around, you can make things clear to them and become partners."

No animal at the Grauls' home was more abused than Zoe, part pit bull, part something else. Some apparent maniac in Brooklyn took her as a puppy and sawed off half of her right front leg and she nearly bled to death. Some kids found her in a pile of rubbish and brought her to the ASPCA. They had to amputate the rest of the leg at the shoulder. She required intense nursing care, and then Tommy and Anne adopted her. Somehow she has forgiven human beings for the unspeakable savagery she suffered.

Today, Zoe, very well adjusted, lives in a mansion built in 1784. It is considered one of the most beautiful in Maryland. She has lots of animal friends to play with in the Grauls' "yard," eighty-six acres of it. Sometimes she gets to ride in a 1962 classic Bentley. She is extremely affectionate and believed to have the fastest tongue in the East. Anne looks at her with obvious love and says, "Living well is the best revenge."

jane bryant quinn

*J*OURNALIST AND SPECIALIST on personal finances Jane Bryant Quinn is unabashedly a cat person. Her husband, David Quinn, is a dog person. But they have reached an accommodation. In fact, it is a fairly obvious one. They have a dog, a German shepherd named Clover, and a cat, fourteen-year-old Sydney. Jane has had as many as five cats at one time, but the canine count is always, somehow, held to one.

Sydney is "queen of the house, and as long as she is here she can rule," Jane says. "She would definitely object to another cat. When she is gone, I'll get two kittens—to start."

Jane recalls the entry of a dog into her life: "Justin was our last child at home. We hadn't had a dog—I was a little afraid of large dogs. But when Justin decided he wanted to go to boarding school, David said he needed another 'son' to fill the void. I said, okay, get a dog—thinking it would take a while. The very next day, he located a German shepherd, which was always his favorite breed. That dog was called Faust, now mourned, and today we have Clover. With a cat and a dog, we're both happy. David has even become extremely fond of Sydney." Jane makes it sound conspirational. It is my experience that cat people are like that.

"Cats are works of art," Jane continues. "They're gorgeous, especially Abyssinians. I have strong aesthetic feelings for cats. I love to look at them. There is nothing cats do that is not graceful. In a cat you have a wonderful work of art that will actually live with you, sit in your lap and purr. Sydney is also a party cat. She comes out for crowds. Guests sitting on the sofa will find her suddenly behind them, purring in their ears. She's rewarding to be with. A cat under a bed is not rewarding. I've had a couple like that.

"I love Clover, our shepherd, who is engaging and affectionate. But you have to be there for a dog all the time. A dog takes as much of you as it can get. You feel guilty if you overlook a dog.

"You can make an arrangement with a cat. It knows when you're busy. If I'm working and Sydney gets too prowly around the keyboard, I put her down and she stays down. When Clover is restless, I have to put her out of the office, period.

Sydney likes to be with me but doesn't demand that I participate or perform—except on weekend mornings and at night, when she pushes at my hand to make me scratch her tummy. That's the arrangement. You can count on it. It's stabilizing.

"As beautiful as Clover is—especially in our kitchen, which, like her, is black, tan and white—she doesn't hold my eye the way a cat does. Aesthetics are important. The fact that you can get on with your life, while the cat is getting on with her life and also presenting all that beauty . . . well, it's very pleasing. Sydney also pleases my heart. Having her sit next to me, purring, while I pat her and read, is peaceful, warm and comforting."

One feels that Jane Quinn needs that. Like many writers on contemporary affairs, she needs an escape technique. She recalls, "I didn't have much animal experience as a child. We had pets briefly, but my mother suffered from allergies, and I must confess that we kids left the care of the pets to her. When I was off on my own, I wasn't even thinking about animals or cats, particularly. But then I went to a friend's house to visit, and [there was] a litter of kittens. I watched them and I played with them and knew that was it. That was what I was missing. I went back later and took a kitten home."

Jane summarizes the difference between cats and dogs as she sees it: "Cats don't push you around the way dogs do. Dogs always want something." But the animal lover in Jane admits her bond to Clover too: "I feel a peaceful love from my cat, but I also feel a strong, affectionate love from our dog. So I return love to both of them. How can you not?"

charles delaney

THIRTEEN-YEAR-OLD Charles Delaney from the Bronx is one of twelve children. He came to Green Chimneys, a very special school in Brewster, New York, knowing little about animals and nothing of how badly he needed their help. It was a revelation, as it is for almost all of the children who have been enrolled in this special place over the last half century. Their life experiences have not prepared the children at Green Chimneys to know that a personal bridge out of themselves can be realized through the animal kingdom, usually through one or two special individual animals. Very quickly, though, they discover a need within themselves to walk across that bridge to a far brighter and more promising world beyond.

For Charles it was horses. He has learned to ride and takes great pride in that fact as well as enjoying the physical and emotional pleasure of the experience. He also likes the work that goes with riding—grooming, mucking out stalls, sweeping the aisles and cleaning the tack.

He rides a horse named Warlock but has a special feeling for Emily and Bob: "I like their colors [Emily is white and Bob is a paint] but most of all I like their eyes. You can tell they're sweet by their eyes. I like to look at their eyes because I know they see me, too. You can tell how horses feel by reading their ears. If they lay their ears back they're angry or something is bothering them. If their ears stick straight up they are wondering about something. Horses are always interested in everything around them. When they put their ears forward they are happy. I like it when they are wondering and when they are happy. I don't like it when they are angry or upset about things. They shouldn't have to be."

Charles often talks to his favorite horses, for he says, "they listen to me. I feel better when I pet a horse. Horses like being around kids, they like it when I'm with them. They especially like it when I pet them on the throat, behind their ears and on the stomach. I like doing that. It makes me feel better, too. I would never take my anger out on a horse."

There are several revealing insights in Charles's comments. He knows he has anger inside of himself and seems to know that he has not always found appropriate outlets for it. He knows and cares that horses would be inappropriate targets for his anger and has promised himself that he would never use them that way. He also says

that horses make him feel better, not good but better. Charles, new to Green Chimneys at the time of this interview, was a child starting on his way across the bridge.

He adds, thoughtfully: "Life would be better if more kids could get to animals, have animals in their lives, they wouldn't get so angry. It really would be better that way."

Because animals and the solace—even guidance—they provide are so new to Charles, one suspects he does not know how many kids already have animals in their lives. He does not know that he is playing "catch-up." The important thing, however, is that he is now in the game, and he has clearly discovered for himself what the rewards can be. He has caught on, and he intends never to let go.

"When I'm done at Green Chimneys, I'm going to be a cop, a mounted cop, and go to work every day on my horse," he says.

Perhaps he will. It would be good for him to succeed at that and, one suspects, good for New York City as well.

skitch henderson

H E MAY NOT LOOK IT when you see him on television or in concert, but Skitch Henderson is as much a farmer at heart as he is a musician. He has lived on a farm for the last twenty-five years. His place in the city, like a baton and a suitcase, is a professional necessity. He and his wife, Ruth, and his Lakeland terrier, Sir Rex, are at home in the country. Sir Rex was named for Skitch's late close friend Rex Harrison.

Skitch has had many animals on the farm. Most of his dogs were large, malamutes, huskies have been favorites, but there were some smaller ones, too.

"I had dachshunds, but I had to give them away when they began hunting my neighbor's chickens. They were feisty little guys."

And there was Ms. Maud, a random-bred dog that lived to be thirteen years old, with whom Skitch had a special relationship.

"We found her when she was a puppy, in a garbage can on First Avenue," Skitch says. "She used to ride on the tractor with me. We were always together."

Then there was Dmitri Kabalevsky, an outsized husky almost as big as a malamute. When he died, Skitch and his family had a ceremony beside his grave. "It was simple and nice," Skitch recalls.

Of all the horses they had when the kids were growing up there is only one left. Morgan (who is a Morgan) is a nice old guy who, at twenty-two, is "just living the good life." Skitch is boarding, that is, providing pasture for, fifty head of cattle. There are about thirty cats on the Henderson spread, walk-ons, all barn cats. There are no house cats at the moment.

Skitch is an animal lover. He admits to it readily and says, "One good thing about having a farm is that your animals can have a natural, outdoor life. They love it. You can tell by watching them. I see animals in the city all the time—on a leash, on pavement—and my heart goes out to them. Maybe I shouldn't feel that way, maybe they just don't know any better and they're really happy. I don't think so, though. I do know that Sir Rex is miserable in New York when I bring him down from the farm. He likes to be with me anywhere I go, but I know he can't wait to get home. Really, he hates the city."

Skitch speaks of himself as a vagabond. He has quite literally lived out of a trunk (or suitcase) for much of his career. His dogs have been an anchor for him, a base.

"It's strange, the animals I have had over the years," he muses. "In Beverly Hills I had dachshunds, two of them, Porgy and Bess. I didn't have twenty-eight cents to my name, but I lived in Beverly Hills and had two dogs."

The kind of life Skitch leads is all pressure all the time, and having a dog is both more difficult and more badly needed than in many more settled lifestyles. I spoke with him about his dogs at nine-thirty at night. He had been rehearsing all day and hadn't finished packing. He was leaving at seven o'clock the next morning with the New York Pops for a ten-day concert tour in Japan. Just talking about his friend Sir Rex seemed to make him unwind. The thought of the little Lakeland terrier is obviously a balm of sorts, no matter what the other demands on him might be.

"I live in a world of critiques," Skitch says. "I have spent my entire life auditioning. But when I go home, to the farm, it is that first five minutes when you come up the drive. You know what is waiting, and then that greeting! I know I am an animal freak. But, really, dogs are so special."

kumiko goncharoff

WHEN KUMIKO WAS GROWING UP in Japan, in Tokyo and other generally urban settings, there were always animals in her home. Her mother was her tutor in the gentle art of loving them and kept dogs, cats, birds and fish, always, no matter where they lived. Kumiko learned the lesson well for she became and has remained an animal lover. A lot of Americans, perhaps, do not realize the degree to which the Japanese love and keep pets. It is as much the norm there as here.

Kumiko has been in the United States for twenty-six years. She became an American citizen late in 1976. For her first eleven years in America she was in the unnatural condition of not owning a pet. Then, on her wedding day, December 31, 1981, Kumiko, now Mrs. Goncharoff, got Neko (that is Japanese for cat), a Russian blue. At the age of fifteen, the beloved cat still lives on in a special place in Kumiko's home and heart.

Kumiko lives an intensely active life. She represents an international clientele for a Manhattan-based real estate firm and deals with very demanding people. She works around the clock because of the time zones she has to accommodate. And what is Neko to Kumiko?

"He is my alter ego, my guru, he helps me stay sane and serene despite my lifestyle and its hectic pace. When I come home, he always greets me—it is very difficult to describe, I don't have the words, but he is very comforting, and I can always count on him. He is a constant in my life."

Kumiko, a product of two very different cultures, speaks English flawlessly. That is not the problem in her difficulty in expressing her feelings. It is that she grew up as a child and young woman in Japan where emotions are not expressed in the same way they are here. It is very different. Things like love and personal needs are more subtly expressed. Putting many things having to do with emotions into words is thought of as limiting and confusing. But Kumiko does say, "Neko helps keep me in touch with who I am. I look at myself in his reflection. His eyes are most revealing and reassuring. He does intensify my awareness of all things."

To talk about Neko as a native Westerner requires Kumiko to switch back and forth between her two cultures. She would rather answer questions about her emotional attachment to her cat with a look, an expression that can be read. She says the Japanese mind has a dread of exaggeration. But pressing valiantly on in an unfamiliar way she adds: "I love him very much. I can't find words to describe the way I feel, to say it properly, but Neko does bring out so many emotions in me because he is so constant, and those emotions include love.

"I don't think I would like to be without a cat again. I am so attached to Neko, he is so much in my life; and he still feels so young to me despite his fifteen years. But I am a realist."

Is Kumiko, then, a cat person? She answers, "No, not really. I have always loved dogs, too. I am a cat-dog person."

However many cultural boundaries have to be dealt with, the final truth remains the same. There is a bond between people and their animals, and although love may be a borrowed word, taken from one emotional context and made to work in another, it does seem to apply. Perhaps one day we will invent another word that will be precise and discrete, designed to work in the world where human beings are bonded to other species.

michael capuzzo

MIKE CAPUZZO, journalist and author, has not yet seen his fortieth birthday, but he has seen four nominations for the Pulitzer Prize. That is more than one nomination for every ten years since his birth, in Boston—a writer and animal lover from the start, it seems certain when you talk to him. In fact he writes like an angel and loves with a gentle intensity that is awesome.

Mike's syndicated column "Wild Things" appears in twenty newspapers with a combined circulation of over ten million readers. His first book was also called *Wild Things* and his second, *Mutts: America's Dogs.*

There are many ways to measure a life's stages and high points. For Mike, one way is by the pets he has owned. Mike's first pet was a collie named Kilty, the second was an Irish terrier named Kerry. Kerry was killed by a car when Mike was ten.

He remembers "feeling such terrible grief. I tried to deny it, to put a cap on it. I think I turned my back on dogs after Kerry died. I was afraid of what they could do to me. We had a cat, though, a big white-and-marmalade cat called Colonel.

"For a boy growing up looking for a role model, 'The Colonel' was a wonderful animal."

But dogs were Mike's great love. One day he was bound to forgive them for the pain he had felt. "I made my reunion with dogs when I was living in Miami. I was a reporter for the *Miami Herald*. We adopted a collie mix and, again, called it Kilty. I was looking for the bond I had lost with my first dog, but this Kilty wasn't really it. I like an in-your-face lapdog, and that just wasn't Kilty."

When the call came, Mike, first wife Jill, Kilty and cat Boonie moved north to a job with the *Philadelphia Inquirer.* Nine days after they arrived, Mike was walking Kilty. It was foggy, and they encountered a free-roaming Ibizan hound. Kilty got away, and the dogs took off. Mike ran after them and eventually found them both dead in front of a church, victims of a city bus. Mike carried Kilty home and knelt down in front of Boonie and tried to explain it to him. If you think about it, that is as logical a way as any to handle grief.

Within two weeks, Mike visited a shelter and met a border collie mix who would become known as Blue. Then another shelter dog, Daisy, a collie–golden retriever mix, came on board.

Mike; second wife Teresa; Mike's two daughters, part-time; Daisy and the latest addition, Texas, live on a farm in New Jersey. Texas is a mastiff-shepherd mix who weighs in at 135 pounds. Wistfully, Mike observes that Texas still has some growing to do. He had only a day to live when a woman from a rescue group handed Mike his leash and said, "If you want him, take him." Mike wanted him.

"The importance of Texas in our lives can't be overstated," Mike says. "He pulled us together. We bought the farm because our 'baby' needed room. Texas is an incredible friend, our protector, an old soul; he is a clown. Sometimes I lie down and use him for a pillow. There is something incredibly comforting about having your pillow breathe in and out beneath you."

Mike believes that his bond with his dogs is enhanced by his being an athlete: "Texas and I really bonded after I began running miles with him. Daisy and I play with a Frisbee by the hour on a football field. These things really cement a relationship."

Mike, a champion of random-bred dogs (he calls them mutts, but with profound affection), observes with bottom-of-the-soul sadness, "We are slaughtering our best friends by the millions. I don't understand it. Dogs have changed my life. I quit my job as a reporter to write books about dogs. They have taught me what is important. When I meet another dog person we share an excitement. It is one of the few socially acceptable ways two virtual strangers can admit to each other that love is the most important thing in the world. Who knows, if we love our dogs there is the possibility we can love each other."

For Michael Capuzzo, humorist and essayist, a generous, gentle man, love really is the most important thing there is.

lainie kazan

LAINIE KAZAN and a bichon frise called Ella (named for Lainie's idol, Miss Fitzgerald) are having an outrageous affair. It is a full-time love-in. To quote Lainie, "She is the sweetest, most loving animal I have ever had. And I have had many, many, many dogs. She goes everywhere with me."

Lainie has, in fact, had dogs all of her life. There was a Manchester terrier when she was a young girl, but her "first, very own dog" was a cross between a bichon and a poodle. "Minerva was so special because she wasn't a family dog. She belonged just to me," Lainie remembers. She also remembers two puppies named Porgy and Bess and an Old English sheepdog she named Nana (in what was perhaps not her single most creative moment).

Another dog came to live with her as the unexpected result of Lainie's appearance on a television program in Australia. Two borzois appeared on the show, and quite naturally Lainie admired them. When the host asked, "Would you like one?" without hesitation Lainie said, "Sure." She didn't give the casual offer any further thought until three months later a very pregnant and very surprised Lainie got a call to come to the airport and pick up her dog.

Other dogs, most acquired more intentionally, include two German shepherds, an apricot poodle, and seventeen years ago a much-beloved sheltie named Sheltie, which might better have been called Miracle. Zsa Zsa Gabor was driving along one of Los Angeles's interminable and potentially lethal freeways when she spotted the little dog, obviously lost, panicked and certainly in danger. Traffic be damned, Zsa Zsa rescued the dog and gave it to Lainie for her daughter—a "present for Jennifer."

Now Ella reigns supreme where so many other dogs have gone before. (A horse, hamsters, turtles, lizards, rabbits and, for just under a week, a tiger cub also went before. The tiger cub, Lainie is quick to admit, was "a very, very bad idea.")

"Ella may not be as bright as some other dogs I have had but she makes up for it in cute. She is so sweet, so gentle and loving, and she has a sense of humor. That's very important to me, a sense of humor!" Lainie says.

"Ella is extremely loving. She is almost like a herding dog. She is always with me, reacting to me. She is very loyal and she makes me laugh. She is so beautiful, with her jet black nose. She has very dark, intense questioning eyes. She can be stubborn, she is like me in that way, she does whatever she wants to do. Ella is not prissy at all. She is game for anything."

As for people who do not make space for Ellas of their own in their lives: "They are missing so much. Being with a dog is a silent pact. They know you in a special way. It softens you. They make you a more available person to not only themselves but to other people. But people who can only communicate with animals, that's not good either, and there are people like that. I feel sorry for them."

Lainie's husband, mentor and friend, Peter Daniels, a pianist, arranger and composer, passed away six years ago. And now that Jennifer has grown up, Ella fills a special space in Lainie's life. "I had a life without animals for about a year, in New York. I did enjoy the lack of responsibility for a while. It was a kind of freedom. But then I needed the comfort, the warmth, I wanted to be at peace, kind of at one with myself and the world, and that's what a dog does for me. I needed to be needed, I guess. Perhaps that's it."

Lainie is a high-pressure performer and actress in concert, in films, on television and on the road. She is always packing, making flight connections, rehearsing, giving interviews, making life work, and she does have a social life many might well envy. But there would apparently be a hole that she would find intolerable if she were doing it by herself. There comes that moment at the end of every day when you are alone, when you say good-bye or good night to the world. The music stops, the applause recedes into the background, the voices dim, the lights fade, the last laugh of the day has been had. But then there is Ella, all white, cute as a button, with a heart as big as all outdoors.

That's how it works for Lainie Kazan for the moment. She has certainly not ruled out the idea of a six-foot-tall, dark-haired man as a good companion, should such be the plans of fate, but with him or without, there will always be room for her Ella.

sam ross

SAM ROSS HAS A PICTURE of himself in a baby carriage with two fox terriers in attendance. Although he doesn't really remember those dogs, he does know that one was named Sunny and that, along with Terry, another wirehair that followed, they helped set his life's course. The influence those dogs had on Sam was to be felt over the next half century by thousands of young people in terrible need.

Sam's father, S. Bernard Ross, was the physician at the Roosevelt Hotel in New York. Sam was born seventeen years after his parents married and was destined to be an only child. The family lived at the hotel, and Sam's fondest memories of those early years are of Terry and a play area he calls the Teddy Bear Cave.

When Sam was five, a Scottie named Lassie appeared, and the two became inseparable. "Lassie was the first dog that I was responsible for. She taught me how to care for dogs. I never forgot," Sam says.

By the time Sam finished kindergarten, his parents had decided that a hotel was not a natural setting for a child, so he was packed off to boarding school in Tarrytown, New York. Shuttling between camps and boarding schools was to be Sam's lot for the rest of his childhood. "I didn't realize until much later that that's what wasn't natural," he reflects. But wherever Sam was to go there would be animals. "The people who had animals were always the nicest people I met," he recalls. "They reached out to me because I was reaching out to them." Sam seems to remember nearly every animal and every animal-related person and event in his life.

When Sam was eight, his parents took him to Europe to celebrate their twenty-fifth anniversary. They, not Sam, fell in love with a school in Switzerland called La Châtaigneraie—The

Chestnut Grove—and Sam was enrolled forthwith. Characteristically, Sam recalls that the headmaster had a wirehaired terrier named Punchy. "I got to care for Punchy, and some draft horses, too." Again, animals.

Sam's stay in Switzerland lasted just under a year. Hitler was making ominous moves in Europe, and Sam's mother came for him. He was enrolled in Greenbrier Military School in Lewisburg, West Virginia. There were dogs, of course, and an array of farm animals. As usual, Sam was the youngest boy in his class. And, as usual, Sam was lonely. He says now, rather naively, "I was always fascinated with animals." It was far more than fascination, as it turns out. Those animals were literally shaping his life in a most remarkable way.

Sam enrolled in the University of Virginia when he was only fifteen and a half years old, and one of his first acts thereafter was to adopt a puppy from the pound. Then came a Scottie and a breeding colony of canaries. "I was too young to drive a car," Sam says. "I didn't drink, I dated high school girls when I could, while my friends were dating college girls. The animals filled in." Somehow, none of this is surprising.

When Sam was nineteen, he graduated from college. He had an idea. He would create a school for young kids, a farm setting, and the kids would care for the animals. "I wasn't sure at first what animals would do for others, but I knew what they had done for me." He talked his father into buying him a seventy-five-acre farm called Green Chimneys. That was in 1947 and it cost $38,500. Sam is still there and the farm is now 150 acres.

Thousands of youngsters have passed through Green Chimneys in the half century since Sam got the idea of mixing kids with animals in a therapeutic modality. Sam remembers, "In my own life there has always been a therapeutic value to connecting with animals, both for me and for the people I work with, the kids. I bond easily with animals and children, and I really like people, but when I was young, I needed companionship and animals gave me that. Now I have plenty." Indeed, Sam Ross does. He and Myra have been married forty-two years. His daughter, Lisa, works, as does Myra, at Green Chimneys. Tragically, his son, David, who also would have worked with his father, died at the age of thirty from Hodgkin's disease after completing his Ph.D. and M.D.

Doctors and social workers come from all around the world to see the miracle of Green Chimneys for themselves. The animals at the farm have been either rescued from abuse or donated. The children, who are from six years old up, have so far flunked life and are referred there by courts, parents or social agencies. There, according to Sam Ross's plan, and in the care of the faculty he has assembled, the kids work with the animals and climb back out of the hole into which an unkind world has dropped them. The rehabilitation success stories among both animals and children are legion and miraculous.

Some three years ago a woman called about a blue-and-yellow macaw that needed a home. A short time later Lola was ensconced in Sam's office. She is still there, and Sam, a world authority on bonding, says of her, "A macaw is a test of your ability to connect. She is very demanding—really a pest—but she is a great companion."

There are now hundreds of animals at Green Chimneys, helping over one hundred resident kids in trouble make it back into the real world. There are forty-one injured birds of prey alone recovering at the farm, but Lola the demanding macaw is something special. She walks around Sam's office with Magic the cairn terrier and Lisa's Scottie, Molly, taking up, one suspects, more of Sam Ross's time than she should. But as it has been since the time of the fox terriers by the baby carriage until now, Sam has an incredible amount of love to share, and animals have always been among the beneficiaries.

paul irwin

PAUL IRWIN IS PRESIDENT of the Humane Society of the United States, one of the most respected organizations in the rapidly expanding community of groups focused on the welfare of animals. In his role as head of a major humane organization, he leads a life full of animals. That is what he and his organization are all about.

As a boy growing up in Brontford, Ontario, Canada, there were family pets, particularly, he recalls, a beagle named Toby. When he got to select his own dog, he gave it the unusual name of Tiglath Pilezer. The biblical name, for such it is, reveals Paul's direction at the time. He was destined for the ministry.

After twenty years of ministry, the Reverend Paul Irwin changed direction and joined the staff of HSUS as a vice president. Today, he is its leader. He is also on the board of the American Bible Society and has a strong opinion about the line from the book of Genesis that says that people shall "have dominion over . . . every living thing that moves upon the earth." He says, "The word 'dominion' in Genesis is disastrous. The concept is—and the words should have been—'have stewardship and be caretakers.' The real platform for religion is based on the concepts of compassion, respect and consideration, not just for human beings, but for all forms of life. If you don't have the animal side you probably don't have the ingredients for human survival, for planetary survival. If you *only* have the human side you denigrate the very basis of our existence. If we are going to have a survivable world for our children and grandchildren we are going to have to have the whole fabric of life intact, respected and treated with compassion and consideration."

Paul and Jean Irwin have been married for thirty-six years and have three grown sons. Their family dogs have included Zack, a black Labrador retriever, and Huxley, a Siberian husky. While those two are gone now, Porsche remains. She was said to be a Chihuahua when Paul first met her nine years ago, but that proved to be not exactly true. She is Chihuahua in part, but there are apparently influences from other cultures and other climes.

The scene was an animal shelter in the American Midwest. It was Paul's fiftieth birthday, and he was spending it touring shelters. He came across a very small puppy who had suffered terribly from frostbite after being abandoned in a snowdrift

during bitter-cold weather. The tiny puppy clung tenaciously to life, but now she faced euthanasia. No one seemed to want to take on the task of nursing her back to health. Paul made up his mind and called Jean back in Maryland to tell her that he had picked out his own birthday gift. Once he got her home, the little dog's climb back to good health was swift. In fact, the name Porsche came from the speed with which the growing puppy ran around in circles in the Irwin household. Paul recollects that Porsche was "faster than any dog I had ever seen. She would skid great curves on the slippery kitchen floor and resume her circuiting at high speed."

Paul reflects on the joy his dogs have brought to his life. "A person like me looks at people who do not understand the glory of companion animals and sees them as impoverished. They have cut themselves off from a spectacular life experience. They have not had the opportunity to be enriched, nurtured and fulfilled through creatures that, because they are not at all like them, introduce them to a whole new and different experience in life."

Despite his intellectual approach to animals and their care, and his high advocacy of the humane ethic, Paul, in the final analysis, is a good, old-fashioned dog lover who says, "We all talk about unconditional love, all the usual statements and observations are almost clichés, now. But very simply, I come home after what may have been a really bad day, and I can be angry, depressed, even despairing, but my dog doesn't react to those emotions or conditions at all. She reacts to me and who I am as a person she loves. It really is unconditional, it offers stability and strength. How can you not love your dog?"

jane alexander

FOR THE LAST TEN YEARS, Jane Alexander has had a recurrent dream. It comes to her often, and she says it may be prophetic. In the dream she is a woman in her mid-eighties—at least thirty years older than she is now. While nothing specific indicates that it's so, she has the impression that her health is good. She is walking across an endless lawn, and on either side of her walk her companions, two black Labrador retrievers. Nothing much happens in this dream of an apparently healthy, elderly woman and her canine friends walking in a time and place of beauty and peace.

In her life as she lives it today, Jane Alexander hikes. She has been a birder for over twenty years and not just at the bird feeders she and her husband, Ed Sherin, maintain at their country home. When she hikes—binoculars and field guide in hand—her companion is six-year-old Cody, a golden retriever. He runs ahead but stops every few hundred feet to check on her, waits for her, then runs on ahead again.

Jane says with a particularly warm and grateful feeling that she has never been without a dog. When she was born, in Boston, her parents had a black standard poodle. Puppies were born, and Jane got her own first dog from that litter. Martini, a white standard poodle, set the course. In time there was a dalmatian, another poodle, German shepherds, a random-bred dog named Muska that is particularly memorable as a traveling companion, a dressing-room dog and another golden named Liberator but called Rator. There were a few cats, too, but Jane is a dog person. She refers to Muska not by the politically correct term "random bred" but as a "mutt." She is not at all defensive about that word, and insists that it is not pejorative.

Jane's life is complex and so is the way she must live it. As head of the National Endowment for the Arts she maintains a res-idence in Washington, D.C. Husband Ed Sherin is in New York, functioning as an executive producer of the celebrated television series *Law and Order*. Their home is north of the city in rural New York State, and they spend their weekends there together.

One of the reasons for choosing a golden retriever, Jane explains, is the ease with which they fit into almost any situation. "Everyone loves them," Jane says, "they can go anywhere." And Cody does. Ed takes him to work every day. He is an office dog and spends hours around the set during filming. Cast and crew members vie for the pleasure of caring for him.

When asked why she has a dog—a large dog—with the busy life she leads, Jane hesitates because "the answers always sound like clichés." When assured that she is talking to another avowed dog person, she replies, "When I look into Cody's eyes it is like meeting an old soul. Cody is my protector, my friend, my hiking companion. He is wonderful to touch, wonderful to come home to." When asked if it would be embarrassing to say that to a non-dog person she acknowledges that it probably would be. She adds, "Pet people, some pet people, at least, are better risk takers, they tend to be more expansive . . . embracing."

There have been many marked successes in the life of Jane Alexander, including her television triumph as Eleanor Roosevelt in *Eleanor and Franklin*, the 1969 Tony for her Broad-way role in *The Great White Hope* (a performance she repeated in Hollywood), the Emmy in 1981 for her part in *Playing for Time* and most recently her appointment as Chairman of the National Endowment for the Arts. Through it all, Jane feels it is normal for her to have a dog near at hand. Taking a new puppy to obedience classes feels right to her. When asked if she will ever be without a dog, she smiles and says no. That's when she tells you about her dream.

mordecai siegal

MORT WAS BORN in South Philadelphia in the early thirties and spent his first eighteen years there in conditions that were less than luxurious. The Siegals were not a Main Line family, it seems.

"My first pet was a box turtle that I found in the street," he says. "What it was doing there I will never know. I was seven, and I really loved that turtle. It was the most wonderful thing that had entered my life. When it died, I found a cigar box and buried it under the only tree on my block. Everything else on the street was cement."

Then a dog entered the life of the future president of the Dog Writers' Association of America. Mort recalls the white spitzlike dog "lived in someone else's yard but he was always running loose in the alley. One day he came up behind me and bit me in the butt, hard, and chased me down the lane. I don't know where I got the nerve but I turned and faced him down. After that, we were pals. He never bit me again. I didn't really own him, but we had a great relationship."

When Mort was eleven, he got his own dog, Tarzan. "Tarzan was a big red random-bred dog, and I really loved him. My father didn't know anything about dogs, really nothing, but one day, he decided that it was time to train Tarzan to walk off lead and that he was the one to do it."

The results were predictable. The big red dog that had brought sunshine and love and so many other values into young Mordecai's life was dead under the wheels of a delivery truck. Mort reflects, "I grieved more for Tarzan than I did for my parents. To this day I can say that nothing has hit me harder. I don't think I have ever again felt pain like that. I never forgave my father. Tarzan was so important to me. He was the only thing that belonged to me. No one else cared for him. The more you get out of a relationship like that, the more at risk you are. When it ends, the pain is so great but it is worth it for as long as it lasts.

"Tarzan left a big mark on the family. At first, no one liked him but me, but then that changed. My Russian-born grandmother lived with us. She was a tough old lady who didn't see why I had to have a dog at all. One morning she got up and poured herself a bowl of cereal but actually it was dog food, something called Growpup. She loved it, and when she told my mother about it, my mother broke up laughing. She had always been dominated by my grandmother but suddenly the roles had switched. My grandmother was adamant that no one else know about her mistake, and as long as my mother held this story over her head she held the power. Tarzan had brought something to my mother that she had always wanted, the leading role in her own home. She loved Tarzan after that."

Like many people who lose their pets to sudden trauma, Mort was afraid to risk having another one after Tarzan died. "I didn't come out of it until I was an adult and, in 1968, married Vicki," he recalls. "She had a cat that she adored, a tough old random-bred named Quentin. Then Vicki bought me a Siberian husky I named Pete, and I was back into animals."

And back he went with a vengeance. He has since become a highly respected and successful writer and editor of books about dogs and cats and is just starting his second term as president of the Dog Writers' Association of America.

Although Mort is president of the DWAA he currently is without a dog since the loss of his cavalier King Charles spaniel, Philadelphia. But he does have a cat. He describes Texas as "a bag of red stripes. He is without a doubt the most intelligent animal I have ever lived with. He is a purebred red classic tabby American shorthair. He has a wonderful, healthy arrogance that you have to admire."

Mort speaks of Texas with a gentle, admiring love. Pets have not only added warmth to the home of Mordecai Siegal, they have given him a distinguished career as well. What more could anyone ask?

maureen mcgovern

*I*N THE EARLY YEARS of Maureen McGovern's lifetime of pet loving, it was an uphill struggle. Without tenacity, the game would have been lost and other things would have to be writ.

"My mother was allergic to cats, and she'd been cornered by a large dog when she was younger and just didn't like them. My aunt lived with us and she wasn't overly fond of dogs, either. So I had to lobby long and hard to get a dog," Maureen says.

Her first remembered pet was a boxer named Tinkerbell, when she was five years old. When she was about nine, she got another boxer, Nicodemus. Both dogs were "given away" (one to the mailman) while she was in school. And so it went during most of her childhood.

Then, when she got married, she and her husband got a German shepherd. "I have always loved shepherds." Maureen smiles. "When we were first getting ready to go on the road, my husband gave our first shepherd away while I was at work with my secretary Joe. Sound familiar?! Then, one day, another shepherd turned up in my dressing room, a gift from fans who were breeders. That was McGillicuddy, McGill for short. Friends raised him, as I was constantly on the road and couldn't take him with me. He was the smartest, kindest, most amazingly human dog I have ever known.

"Seventeen years later I was in Naples, Florida, touring with Mel Tormé. I fell in love with a Yorkie—it was literally love at first sight—and the Tormés urged me to buy him. They had a Yorkie of their own and so did our bus driver. 'Go on, bring him along,' they all said, so Nicodemus (the second) joined our tour. His full name is Nicodemus Bebop Dickens. Mel is his godfather; he added the Bebop to his name."

But it didn't stop there. It seldom does with truly ardent dog people.

Maureen continues, "Nicky and I were on the road, as usual, and we were back in Florida—Sarasota. We bumped into a couple walking down the street, they were Yorkie breeders, and they had a baby carriage with a litter of eight puppies in it. We talked and I went my way, thinking about those adorable puppies. In a little while I turned a corner and bumped into them again . . . kismet! That's when I got Rocky.

"I love my little guys. When I recently went to Africa and Southeast Asia I couldn't take them with me, and I missed them terribly. But they *love* my housekeeper, and he takes care of them for me when I am on tours outside the U.S. They're perfectly happy to be in their own beds—as long as he's around if I'm not."

For Maureen there do not seem to be any limits to pet owning. "Nicodemus is very social," she says. "He goes to the movies with me. He loves to party. He even went to President Clinton's inauguration. I am sure he was the only dog there. His bag went through the metal detector, and he was searched for weapons and passed on in. He's my politically correct puppy—he's even been in a pro-choice march."

There is no doubt about the role her dogs play in Maureen McGovern's life. As with so many performers, life is one long journey. As much as 80 percent of her time may be spent on the road; 75 percent of the time the Yorkies go along.

"I love these puppies [Nicky is five years old, Rocky—actually Rockwell Doowop St. Armande—is eighteen months, but Maureen still refers to them as "puppies"] with all my heart. Those sweet little faces, I really don't know how to put it into words. They are comforting, they are very, very funny, they make me laugh. Rocky was a kick boxer in another life, and Nick is very much a gentleman. It took a year for them to get along. It was a year to the day after I got Rocky, and they suddenly started to play together. No matter how bad my day gets, when they come running with those little faces . . . well! If I do say so myself, they are exceptionally beautiful dogs. There is wisdom in their eyes. They have been here before. I know it. They are so like people—children—with their own distinct personalities, traits and habits."

When Maureen McGovern talks about her dogs it is like reading James Joyce without the brogue and the steamier memories—it is a stream of consciousness that is all about love and comfort.

dick schaap

*E*VERYTHING ABOUT DICK SCHAAP is energetic. Energy, one suspects, must be his middle name. He is a theater critic and a sports correspondent for ABC, covering everyone from Shoeless Joe Jackson to ageless Carol Channing. He has written thirty-one books on subjects ranging from murder to comedy, from politics to sports, with the obvious overlaps. He has six children, five grandchildren, but it did take him three wives to get it right. He is never without a joke, and even if you have heard it before, you listen because the style and the energy level will make it new.

All of that and enter Bandit, the only member of the Schaap family with more pizzazz than Dick himself. That family today consists of Dick, Mrs. Schaap, the former Trish McLeod of Scotland, daughter Kari, fourteen, and son David, ten. The marriage, now fifteen years old, had, until recently, everything but a dog. Dick was born in Brooklyn and has lived in that borough and Manhattan, in Queens, on Long Island, in New Jersey and Connecticut. But it is a life that has been centered on Gotham, and that is not always compatible with a canine's needs. Because there were always kids, there were pets—cats, ferrets, fish and turtles, lots of cats. Dick lived with them all but did not bond with any of them. He is, by self-definition, a dog person.

There were a couple of dogs in Dick's past. First, there was Ginger. But Dick grew up on dog stories featuring handsome collies, so along came Max, a regal specimen of that breed. Dick was then editor of *Sport* magazine and often walked back to the office after dinner, with Max decorously by his side. It gave Max his evening exercise, but there was more to it than that. The walk home from the office took them past the Blue Angel night-club, and the club's owner happened to be a friend of Dick's. There was usually a brief visit. On an average night, Max enjoyed the remains of six or seven steaks. The club featured a sparkling transvestite show whose cast members fussed endlessly over Max and insisted on calling him Maxine.

Max was admired by others, too. One in particular Dick will never forget. The date was July 4, 1976, the day of the tall ships. Max and Dick were walking past the Regency Hotel when a well-appointed lady emerged and insisted on admiring and patting Max. She commented on his regal nature and splendid demeanor. After she left them, the doorman pointed out to Dick that the lady entering her limousine was Her Serene Highness Princess Grace of Monaco.

Max was regal and well mannered but not too much more than that. "He was so good looking," Dick recalls, "that he really didn't have to do anything, just stand there." That was in the 1970s, when the corner of Park Avenue and Sixty-first Street was a haven for some of New York's most expensive short-term company. Max befriended many of the ladies. He and Dick normally passed that corner of negotiable charms on their walks, and handsome Max visited briefly with his friends of the evening. One can detect more than a little of Damon Runyon in the combination of Dick Schaap and Max Collie abroad in New York in the night.

Max had been long gone when Dick's son, David, started making the "Why can't I have a dog?" sounds that are normal for an active ten-year-old boy. Dick is sensitive to kids, and besides, Trish, a real dog person, was making the same kind of sounds. They got Dick's attention, and he called a friend at the ASPCA, looking for another dashing character like Max. The planets were in good positions, a dog named Bandit was available for adoption.

You look at Bandit and say, "Thy name is dog." Bandit is everydog. His parents were crossbreeds, and in all likelihood their parents were, too. He has none of the splendor that Max had, but all of the personality that Max lacked. Bandit is, in fact, Mr. Personality and has bonded not just with Dick but with Trish and the kids, as well. He sleeps in Dick's bed and, in a nice way, is jealous of any attention Dick and Trish show each other. Trish and David, after a very well orchestrated campaign, got their dog. But Mr. Energy *found* his. There, beside the fast lane, waiting for someone with the right energy level and a very big heart to come along, was Bandit. By mutual agreement the bond was almost instantaneous. It was a done deal. The rest, surely, will be part of the history of the city they call the Capital of the World.

judy collins

*J*UDY COLLINS had a very close friend when she was a little girl. The friend was Fluffy, a gray Persian cat that was her first pet.

Judy says, "She and I were very close. I woke up one morning and Fluffy was on my bed, as usual, but she was surrounded by a litter of wet kittens. I remember calling for help. I cried out that Fluffy had fallen apart."

There was a whole parade of pets in those early years. Chris, a parakeet, stands out. She recalls, "I still miss him to this day. His wings were just a little too long, they needed clipping. Someone left a door open. It was winter but he flew out. It was many days before we found his body. I was devastated."

Judy grew up in a family of animal lovers. Her parents, a brother and a sister were all afflicted. She remembers a cocker spaniel named Koko, a tortoiseshell cat named Priscilla, who was found on a beach in Oregon—the list went on and on. The pets seem to have come in waves. At one point, the family had five cats. In addition to Priscilla, there was Hoby, a Siamese; Jam, another tortoiseshell; Clyde, an orange cat; and Spotted, a tricolor. They were all about the same age, and when they reached sixteen or seventeen, it was over. Within a year they were all dead. Judy and her husband, designer Louis Nelson, replaced those cats—if that can ever actually be done—with Ribbons, Bows and Ruffles. And there were dogs, too— huskies. Kolya joined the family in Colorado, and Smoky came on board in New York. Each was loved in turn, and each loved back in its own way.

The influence of all this was naturally played out with Judy's son, Clark. He added fish, hamsters and lizards that Judy found to be "interesting little animals."

What all this means, of course, is that Judy Collins is one of the great animal lovers of our time—a heavy-duty, industrial-strength animal lover. "I would have horses if I could," she says; and then, again, "I really love horses.

"One of the first successes I had as a child was when I befriended a really antagonistic, cantankerous old billygoat. I probably sang to him." Even then she knew the power of music: "Animals do love music, you know. Really, they do," she insists.

"I mistrust people who don't like animals. There is something wrong with them. I don't understand it, but I instinctively mistrust them. As for me, I'm a cat and bird person indoors, but if I am out, I am a horse and dog person."

Today, Judy shares as much of her life as possible with two "wonderful cats. Sunshine is a black Persian and Midnight—Mr. Personality himself—is a white Persian.

"Oh, God, I love them," she says. "When I come in they roll over to greet me, they give me all kinds of signs that they love me, too. In my life they are so essential, they are so comforting. I love to play with them, I love to interact with them. They sleep on my bed, they are really so social, they love to be in on the party. I have the feeling that the animals you have pick up on your personality. I know these two think of me as their mother. There is a strong patterning effect I have had on their personalities."

Could it be otherwise for the singing lady from out West—Seattle, Denver and Los Angeles? Probably not. Wouldn't years of fame and accomplishment be enough? There aren't that many Americans, after all, who don't know who Judy Collins is and what she has meant in her own time. But for Judy, it wouldn't be enough. She reflects, "I am not sure that life without animals would be worth living. I can't imagine what it would be like to live like that, with so much missing." Fortunately, Judy Collins doesn't have to imagine the dreadful petless state. She obviously will not have to deal with it.

brian kilcommons

DOGS HAVE BEEN AT THE CENTER of Brian Kilcommons's life from the very beginning. He grew up with them, and they have literally given him the good life he leads.

"In my career as a dog trainer, dogs have enabled me to make a living at what I value most, learning about dogs, working with them, loving them. They have made my life so very much better. It is all about and because of dogs," says Brian.

"That is how I met Sarah and most of my best friends. Dogs seem to string things together, love affairs and long-term friendships. Anywhere you go in the world, dogs are the common denominator."

Today, Brian and his wife and coauthor, Sarah Wilson, also a dog trainer, live on a farm north of New York with five dogs, three cats, two horses, forty sheep and twenty chickens. The forty sheep, Brian is quick to point out, "are for wool only."

Brian's family had a dog when he was born, a random-bred terrier called Irish. When he was fifteen, Brian got his first personal dog. Somehow it mattered that it was not his family's dog, but his own. The dog's name was Tara—from the name of the seat of ancient Irish kings—and he was a vizsla. When Brian discovered that Tara was also the name of a goddess he changed the dog's name to T.

Arguably, Brian is the best dog trainer in the country, or at least he is in the front rank with the very best of them, as good as they come. His secret?

"Empathy—both with the owner and the dog. I want it to work for both of them, and I can see where each is coming from. You have to be able to look at a dog and understand what is going on in its mind and behavior. I think I have special insight. I can detect and relate to fear and aggression. I can feel it."

And well he might. He grew up in a violent and cruel family environment and feels it to this day. That's one of the reasons the vizsla named T was so important to him. He has hardly ever been without a dog of his own since then, although now he does share his dogs with Sarah.

Brian reflects, "That history of mine is one of the reasons I can sense things about dogs and people—any sign of fear or violence. When I first got into the field I saw so much abuse going in the name of training that I rejected it—all abuse."

As much as he knows about dogs, Brian is endlessly amazed by them.

"They are constantly surprising me with how intelligent they are. Each one is unique. It is not true that a dog is a dog is a dog. They are all individuals. Their ability to spring back after unbelievable mishandling, their sense of humor, their ability to bring us back to everyday life—it is all amazing. Regardless of what goes on in our lives, who we are, dogs are great levelers. They are simply not impressed. They want us for who we are, not what we are.

"I dearly love dogs, I do the best I can to fight for them and how they should be treated. They need advocates."

One can feel how badly Brian wants to give something back to his lifelong friends. His indebtedness is acknowledged without reserve or embarrassment.

"We are arrogant in the ways we approach our dogs—on human terms," he says. "We don't appreciate them. If you study them, their ways of learning are exquisite."

Not many people can express so clearly their sense of debt, or state so simply their resolve to do everything possible to make things right—without abuse and without violence. For Brian Kilcommons, living with a dog is an art form. It is a perfect blend, it is life in balance.

tommy tune

TOMMY TUNE IS AT THAT POINT in his career as a performer and
director/choreographer when the right thing for him to do would be to star in a
musical in London's West End and then bring the show home to America in triumph.
His agent is—relentlessly—urging him to do it. Producers in England are offering
him the earth, and his many English fans are clamoring. He could have things pretty
much the way he wants them. But his answer is calm, quiet, unequivocal: "No way,
José." (Tommy is a Texan.)

The answer as to why this elongated Broadway star says no to what logic
dictates is right is simple. His name is Ophelio, Ophie to his friends. If he performed
in England, Tommy would have to leave his diminutive Yorkshire terrier behind. The
British authorities are so paranoid about rabies that they would require that Ophie
undergo six months in a quarantine station, or stay home. Tommy repeats, "No way,
José. I'm not leaving my dog behind."

Tommy's father trained horses back in Texas. Tommy had "an old bay geld-
ing" named Big John that he loved, but there were never any dogs. Ophie, a gift from
a friend a few years back, is his "one and only dog."

Tommy was surprised at what happened once Ophie arrived. He says, "I
thought my life was set, then this little thing turned it upside down." Tommy had
thought about having a dog, but until he had star status—had a penthouse and
people to help him—he didn't feel he had the right to own a dog. He didn't feel he
could care for one properly. He started out as a choreographer in summer stock and
then hit as a performer. Before he became a star he had to share dressing rooms with
others, and it didn't seem fair to bring a dog along. Now, Ophie travels everywhere
Tommy goes, with his own half-price ticket. He is perfect for a star on tour.

Tommy now thinks of his life as B.O. and A.O., before and after his tiny mite
of love made his entrance. He has recently completed his memoirs. He says the mood
of the writing actually changes at that before-and-after break point in his life. Tommy
says, "There's a whole spectrum of emotions I was simply unaware of before. I never
dreamed of what it could be like. Now, Ophie's the center of attention. His is pure
unconditional love." Tommy is fascinated by the fact that something can live with
absolutely no other task but love, to give love, to be loved. He says, "I've heard that

people come to look like their dogs. I hope so. I would love to look like him." There is a significant size disparity to be dealt with here, but that doesn't seem to matter.

Whether Tommy is on Broadway or on tour, Ophie hangs out in the dressing room. He quickly learns the show's routine and the order of scenes. He stands guard over the rack that holds Tommy's costumes, arranged to facilitate fast changes. He gets into the routine and likes things kept as they are.

When the routine changes, Ophie doesn't keep his displeasure to himself. Once, Tommy was in Seattle with *Bye, Bye Birdie*. It was the night of the Tony Awards. On a live hookup, Tommy was to break from the stage show and accept two Tonys, for directing and as a choreographer. The audience loved being in on the live TV show and seeing "their" star being so honored. Ophie didn't. The fast switching for television and the theater production involved costume changes out of order, and Ophie nearly had a nervous breakdown. Tommy recalls, "The poor little thing went absolutely nuts." Tommy is Ophie's star, and Ophie doesn't like anyone interfering with routines once he has accepted them. "Watch what happens when you try to leave," Tommy warned, and he was right. Ophie barked up a storm. Guests become routines, too.

One routine Ophie seems to enjoy more than any other comes at Christmas and on birthdays. Ophie loves to open Tommy's gifts. It doesn't matter what's inside. The ribbons and the paper are what count, and Ophie goes fairly mad with excitement when the brightly wrapped packages appear.

Into almost every facet of Tommy Tune's life, Ophie has inserted his energy, his demands and offerings of love. He and his master, who is about twenty-five times as tall as he is, have struck up a seemingly perfect relationship. Tommy will direct and choreograph the shows, and star in them, and Ophie will guard his costumes and love him no matter what. But it isn't all one sided, Ophie will let Tommy love him, too. And they both will forego London and do all that loving right here where the authorities don't worry about little Manhattan penthouse dogs carrying dreaded diseases into the countryside. Tommy doesn't know of a single case of a dog or anybody else catching rabies in a Broadway dressing room.

susan goldstein

THERE IS NO MISTAKING the focus of Susan Goldstein's life. With their three children grown, Susan and her husband, Bob, a veterinarian, coedit a newsletter called *Love of Animals: Natural Healing for Your Pets.* Susan is the founder of Earth Animal, a retail store in Westport, Connecticut, that sells all-natural products. Susan calls it "a complete department store for animals, people and the environment."

Susan and Bob have researched, developed and marketed a number of natural products for nutrition and for flea and tick control. Susan takes the same approach to these matters that her husband does in the veterinary practice they co-own, a holistic one.

The Goldstein household presently includes three dogs, Jack the boxer and two Pembroke Welsh corgis. Jack is the only dog the Goldsteins have purchased in their three decades together. The other thirty or so were all rescues. Also in residence are Ellie, a rescued cat; a couple of zebra finches, a species that Susan raises; and one incredible sun conure named Mac, short for MacMillan. Mac was domestically bred, but his kind is native to tropical America.

Mac is very protective of his family, very loving and obviously extraordinarily bright, but he has a peculiarity: He bites just about everyone who comes within range of his beak, except Susan. Susan says, "Mac is a man-eater. I really did not do my homework. I bought with my heart, not my intellect. I didn't socialize him enough. He's very aggressive with strangers and people he doesn't approve of." Birds, apparently, can feel jealousy and resist sharing the people they claim as their own. Susan continues, "We cage him when strangers are here. He really cannot be trusted. Anyone in the room at any distance may be attacked. He has broken the skin on my daughter and my sister. He loves my husband but won't tolerate him being around me without biting him. He controls Bob with pinches but he will not break the skin. He knows how much pressure to apply before cutting him some slack." It is interesting that Susan admits she would never tolerate that behavior from a dog or cat, but she will from Mac.

Mac doesn't just use his beak on people. "He carves up my house!" Susan exclaims. "He'll fly to a tree we have for him when I ask him to. He does not carve where he is prohibited. When I come home, I ask him to show me his work, and he will. He will fly to what he is working on. We give him blocks of unbleached softwood, and he carves them, too."

What, exactly, does Susan mean by "carve"? All members of the parrot family will shred wood. It is a common form of recreation and beak maintenance. But Susan insists that Mac works purposefully on designs and has recently done a wave— something this captive-bred bird could have seen while with the family on trips to the beach in Montauk, at the eastern end of Long Island, New York.

Does all of this Mac lore sound excessively anthropomorphic? Susan responds, "I can't help it. It is really happening." Mac's art is not his only human characteristic, he is a great companion to Susan. Mac, Susan explains, really wants to please. He is responsive to verbal commands and tries to help her make the bed. Susan is a morning person and Mac is a morning conure. They both get up at 4 A.M. and watch the sunrise. They listen to music together and also meditate—it is an amazing relationship. When Susan comes out of her meditative state, she usually finds Mac, her beautiful feathered companion, with his eyes closed. One wonders if he really is making his mind go blank or if he is using that time to conjure up new conure designs.

molly o'neill

MOLLY O'NEILL grew up in a family of animal lovers. They lived on five acres, and her parents raised Great Pyrenees—an experienced dog-owner's dog. Molly had five younger brothers and learned when she was quite young what responsibility and nurturing mean.

Off on her own, Molly didn't think a busy young career woman should have a dog in Manhattan, so she settled down with two cats. She has had them for fifteen years now. But in that time along came husband-to-be Arthur, and he already had a dog, a bearded collie named Herschel—a little boy, Molly insists, in a bearded collie suit. Then came Betty Lou, another beardie—really Blanche Dubois, Molly says. And then Phoebe, a champion-quality beardie now being shown under the name of Llanfair Field of Heaven.

A dog must want to show (loving to show is even better). People who know show dogs can tell you that a dog that doesn't want to show won't stand a chance. Dog owners know that conformation to the rules of showing is only part of it, mostly it is will, passion for the sport and style.

"Phoebe loves it," observes Molly. "She struts around the ring. Her feet don't seem to touch the ground. She shows off. She is an athlete and can clear a six-foot fence with ease. At home, she is a thirty-seven-pound lapdog. She flies through the air and lands on you. It can be surprising. I am deeply bonded to Phoebe. She sleeps under my desk when I am writing, often with her head on my foot.

"I really believe that you define yourself when you find your opposite. For example, I am not a Park Avenue socialite. But I might not know that until I have lunch with some Park Avenue socialites. In the same way, having dogs reminds me that I am human. That's my response to them. It is my job, my place in life to see to it that they have their cookies at three in the afternoon. If I am going to be away on a book tour I get them clipped before

I go so they won't miss our grooming routine. Being human doesn't just give me power, it gives me these responsibilities."

Molly is exceedingly busy and leads a full life in her various roles as wife, mother to a five-year-old, food columnist for *The New York Times Magazine* and cookbook author with her own test kitchen as well as the family loft apartment to manage. But she is also a dog owner, and that is always figured in as a very important factor.

"The affection you receive from beardies is remarkable and intuitive," she says. "When I was sick, Phoebe would come over and put her head on my lap or a paw on my shoulder, just for the feeling of contact. You realize you are a sentient being because your dog knows you are and reminds you of it.

"With cats, it's always a deal. You give them their food twice a day, and clean water, you pet them when you want to, and they'll let you pet them if they're in the mood. You keep their cat box clean, you take them to a vet when they need it, and they'll sit on your lap. It is more of a bargain with cats than the liquid exchange there is with a dog."

She reflects on what relating to an animal can tell about a person: "If Arthur hadn't been an animal lover I would have had deep suspicions. I would certainly have had my doubts. My cats are character judges. When I was dating a lot and a guy came back here, my cats decided right away who they liked. They even attacked guys, and it was good-bye right then and there. The first time Arthur came here both of my cats climbed into his lap. It was a sign."

Taking responsibility for a pet is not something to be taken lightly. Molly laughs. "Having pets is not free. The benefits are huge but it is costly. The veterinarian, the time they require—financially and emotionally it is anything but free. But it is not onerous, these are things you want to do, want to give."

For Molly, her bond to her dogs is a stabilizing factor in her busy life. She sums it up: "One important thing they do, dogs make you wake up and realize that you are not the center of the universe."